# PRACTICAL ELECTRICAL Manual

## Martynn Randall

**The Haynes Manual for chassis electrical systems**

Haynes Publishing
Sparkford, Nr Yeovil, Somerset BA22 7JJ England

Haynes North America, Inc
861 Lawrence Drive, Newbury Park, California 91320 USA

Editions Haynes
4, Rue de l'Abreuvoir
92415 COURBEVOIE CEDEX, France

Haynes Publishing Nordiska AB
Box 1504, 751 45 Uppsala, Sweden

A book in the Haynes Service and Repair Manual Series

Printed in the USA

**ISBN 1 84425 267 1**

**British Library Cataloguing in Publication Data**
A catalogue record for this book is available from the British Library

While every attempt is made to ensure that the information in this manual is correct, no liability can be accepted by the authors or publishers for loss, damage or injury caused by any errors in, or omissions from, the information given.

*(4267-160)*

# Introduction

## Introduction

Not too long ago, the average automotive electrical system consisted of a battery, a dynamo, a few motors and a bunch of switches, relays, fuses and lights. Not any more.

In the last two decades, car electrical systems have become increasingly elaborate. The rate at which electrical/electronic systems are evolving outpaces development on other parts of the car. As you're probably aware, there's a lot of electrical complexity in even the simplest new cars.

The best automotive electricians are sometimes baffled by modern electrical systems, and you, the home mechanic, may not feel qualified to work on them.

We at Haynes think we can restore your confidence. In this book, we have tried to take a practical approach to diagnosing and repairing problems related to the chassis electrical system. You'll find a minimum of electrical theory and a maximum of diagnostic and repair information. You don't have to be an electrician to use this book, and you don't have to spend a king's ransom on special tools and test equipment; the equipment you'll need to perform the procedures in this book should pay for itself after the first few repairs.

As with all automotive work, the keys to success are patience and clear, careful thinking. Obviously, the procedures in this book can't lead you step-by-step through every electrical problem you'll encounter. Chapters 1, 2 and 3 are designed to give you a basic understanding of automotive electrical systems and introduce you to logical troubleshooting procedures. This knowledge will prepare you to deal with all types of electrical problems. Even if you've done some work on electrical systems before, it's a good idea to review the information in these Chapters, especially the information on test equipment in Chapter 3.

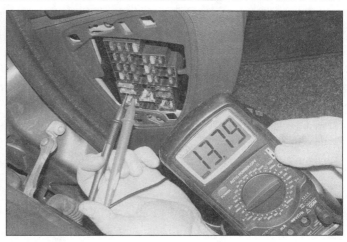

In Chapters 4 to 8, you'll find detailed troubleshooting procedures as well as component replacement and overhaul information for starting, charging, lighting, gauge and accessory circuits. The individual procedures in these Chapters discuss any special equipment needed to carry out the procedure.

Since this book cannot detail all variations of all vehicles, we recommend you supplement the information in this book with the Haynes Service and Repair manual written for your particular vehicle. Using these two books, some patience and a minimum of test equipment, you should be able to handle most repairs on chassis electrical systems.

**Caution: The procedures in this manual are written for vehicles with negative-earth electrical systems. Some older (mostly British) vehicles have positive-earth systems. If you're working on a vehicle with a positive-earth system, you may have to reverse references to 'positive' and 'negative' in some procedures.**

# Introduction

## Acknowledgements

Thanks are due to ECS Ltd. for the supply of the Parking Distance Sensor Kit detailed in Chapter 8.

ECS Ltd.
PO Box 534
Horsham RH13 9WJ
United Kingdom
www.parking-sensor.co.uk

Thanks are due to Robert Bosch Limited for the use of illustrations, and Draper Tools Limited for workshop tools.

**While every care is taken to ensure that the information in this manual is correct, no liability can be accepted by the authors or publishers for loss, damage or injury caused by any errors in, or omissions from, the information given.**

# *Basic automotive electricity*

Electricity and the car

What is electricity?

Measuring electricity

Electrical circuits

Circuit malfunctions

Multiplexing and networks

## Electricity and the car

Without electricity, modern cars could not function. Electrical devices start your car, charge the battery, monitor the engine, play music, roll the windows up and down, lock the doors, adjust the mirrors, wipe the windscreen, illuminate the road, tell other drivers when you're stopping or turning and perform a host of other tasks *(see illustration)*. You probably never give one of these components a second thought, unless, of course, it malfunctions . . .

People spend their entire lives studying the mysteries of the phenomenon known as electricity. Unless you're planning to become an electrical engineer, we assume you don't have the time to do that. You want to learn enough about electricity and electrical theory so you can understand how the components and systems on your vehicle function. That's this Chapter's focus.

*This (greatly simplified) wiring harness illustrates the car's dependence on electricity for nearly everything*

# Chapter 1

## What is electricity?

No one actually knows, but after several hundred years of trying to figure it out, we do know some of its characteristics:

*It has positive and negative charges*
*It's invisible*
*It can be controlled*
*It flows (in a complete circuit)*
*It can be stored.*

You may remember something about positive and negative charges from school science lessons. And you probably have at least a vague sense of some of the other characteristics of electricity. Lets review some of those ideas briefly.

### Polarity

Remember those experiments you did with magnets in school science class? Every magnet has a North pole and a South pole. On some magnets, these poles are marked + (positive) and – (negative). If you place the + pole of one magnet near the – pole of another magnet, they attract each other. If you put both + poles or both – poles near each other, they repel each other. We call this attraction of opposites and repulsion of likes polarity. Polarity causes electrons (and thus electrical current) to act as it does.

### Electrons

Why is electricity invisible? Because it operates on an atomic level. Atoms are the building blocks of the universe; everything is made of atoms. They can't be seen because they're very small. It would take millions of them to dot each i in this sentence. Amazingly, atoms themselves still aren't the smallest parts of matter. Each atom is composed of particles – protons, neutrons and electrons. Protons have a positive charge, electrons have a negative charge and neutrons, as the name implies, have no charge. Electrons, like tiny planets, orbit around the atom's nucleus (composed of protons and neutrons). They are held in their orbit because they are attracted to the positively charged protons in the nucleus (remember from our earlier discussion that positive and negative charges attract each other) (*see illustration*).

In the atom of a good conductor (like copper), some of the electrons are not strongly attracted to the protons in the nucleus and are free to float from one atom to another. If an extra electron is introduced into the orbit of an atom, one of the electrons already there is forced to leave, since there is now an excessively negative charge in the atom. We can harness this phenomenon, known as electron drift, to produce electrical current. The trick is to put excess electrons into orbit in the atoms of a conductor.

So where do these excess electrons come from? On cars, they come from the battery or alternator. We will discuss these two components in depth in later chapters, but for now, just think of them as devices that produce zillions of excess electrons. At one terminal of the battery, or alternator,

*Electrons closest to the nucleus are called 'bound electrons' because they're tightly controlled by the nucleus – electrons farthest from the nucleus are referred to as free electrons because they're free to leave*

there are too many electrons; at the other, there aren't enough. Attach a copper wire between the two terminals of a battery or an operating alternator and free electrons start pushing into the copper wire. What was random electron drift begins to assume a pattern of more or less continuous movement. As long as there are too many electrons behind, and not enough ahead, the electrons travel in a semi-orderly way in one direction. This directional flow of electrons in the wire is called electrical *current*.

### Current flow and conductors

Current flow only occurs in materials with lots of free electrons. Such materials are called conductors. Copper is a good conductor, but it isn't the only one. Other metals, including aluminium, lead and even gold are sometimes used as electrical conductors.

When electrons flow through a conductor, the effect of the flow is available instantaneously at the other end of the conductor. The speed of the electrons is actually less than a few inches per second, but the energy applied to one end of the circuit is transmitted at the speed of light. The way it works is illustrated by the following example:

Imagine several billiard balls placed in a line, each touching the next. Drive another ball into the first ball in line and what happens? A ball simultaneously pops off the other end of the line (*see illustration*).

*Current travels at the speed of light using a principle that's similar to this billiard-table example – think of the force from the cue ball as voltage and the balls striking each other as current flow*

Electrons behave in the same way, only much faster. This movement of electrons along a conductor is called *amperage* and is directly related to the voltage (the electrical pressure that causes the current to flow) applied to the conductor.

## Resistors

In some materials, like iron, nickel and nichrome, electron drift isn't as active as it is in a good conductor. When a free electron drifts to another atom, some of its energy is absorbed, and the electron pushed out has less energy than the one that displaced it. Materials made of these atoms are called resistors because, even though they conduct, they resist (slow down) current flow.

## Insulators

In some materials, there's no electron drift at all, so they can't conduct electricity. These materials are sometimes referred to as dielectric, but more often are simply called *insulators*. Typical insulating materials include air, rubber, glass, wood, plastics, bakelite and porcelain. Note that insulators are all some sort of non-metallic material; conductors and resistors are usually made of metal.

## Semiconductors

Semiconductors, or solid-state devices, are the basic building blocks of electronic circuits. They're made from a material (usually silicon) that doesn't conduct in its pure form, but will behave like a conductor under certain conditions.

## Measuring electricity

So far, we've been talking about electricity from a theoretical standpoint. But when you're working on your car, it's critical that you know the relationship between voltage, amperage and resistance. We've already touched on two of these three terms. Now let's define them.

## Volts

Volts are units of electrical pressure – how much pressure is pushing the electrons through the circuit. The symbol used for volts is V. Smaller voltages are measured in millivolts (1/1000th of a volt); larger voltages are measured in kilovolts (1,000 volts).

## Amps

Amps, or amperes, are units of electron flow – how fast the electrons are passing through the conductor. The symbol for Amps is A. Smaller current flow is measured in milliamps (ma) (1/1,000th of an amp).

## Ohms

Ohms are units of resistance – how much the conductor or resistor resists the flow of electric current. The symbol for ohms is the Greek letter Omega ($\Omega$). Smaller resistances are measured in milliohms (m$\Omega$) (1/1,000th of an ohm). Larger resistances are measured in megohms (M$\Omega$) (1,000 ohms).

### Ohm's Law

In the early 1800s, a German physicist named George S. Ohm described the link between voltage, amperage and resistance in a simple electrical circuit. He said that:

The current in a circuit is directly proportional to the applied voltage and inversely proportional to the resistance in the circuit.

It is important that you understand this relationship between volts, amps and ohms. If you study Ohm's Law, as it's called, carefully, you will see that it can be broken down into three simple statements:

1 *When the voltage goes up or down, current flow also goes up or down (as long as the resistance stays the same).*
2 *When resistance goes up, current goes down (as long as voltage stays the same).*
3 *When resistance goes down, current goes up (as long as voltage stays the same).*

Unless you'll be designing circuits, that's all you really need to know about Ohm's law. And you'll be able to understand what any voltage, resistance or amperage is telling you about the other two values.

## Electrical circuits

Now that you know a little about how electricity behaves in general, let's look at how it behaves in a typical car circuit. First, we need to look at what makes up a circuit. Then we'll describe how it works and discuss the three basic types of automotive circuits.

In its simplest terms, the circuit is the basis for current flow. Without a circuit, there can be no current flow. The circuit is also what ties the components of an electrical system together. Without a circuit to connect them, electrical components would be just that – components. When they're connected in a circuit, they become a system.

For a circuit to exist, two conditions must be present:

1 *There must be a complete, unbroken path through which the current can flow. It must be able to flow from the source of the voltage, through all the various wires, connectors, switches and components and back to the voltage source. When this condition exists, the circuit is said to have continuity.*
2 *There must be a difference in voltage between two points of the circuit. In automobiles, these points are the two battery terminals. This difference is called potential.*

Automotive circuits have two sides: The feed (power) side (attached to the positive [+] battery terminal on most vehicles), and the return (earth or ground) side (attached to the negative [–] battery terminal on most vehicles). In a

*A complete circuit has a feed or power side (the conductor) and a return path to the voltage source (the battery) – the device being powered (the load) is the dividing point between the two sides of the circuit*

Note: Ground is another term for Earth

1654-1-1.4 HAYNES

simple circuit that has only one load (component being powered by the current flow), the load is the dividing point between the two sides *(see illustration)*.

## Single-wire circuits

Cars normally use *single-wire* circuits. They have a feed wire to each load, but do away with the return wire back to the source. Instead, components are connected, individually or in groups, to the chassis/body, which acts as a big return conductor back to the battery. This chassis return path is known as *earth* or *ground*. The battery itself is connected to earth/ground by cables from the negative terminal (on most vehicles) to the chassis/body.

## Voltage difference

Before we look at the three basic types of circuits found on cars, there are two other concepts you should understand – voltage difference (which we've briefly touched upon already) and voltage drop.

Look at the accompanying illustration *(see illustration)*. The switch is open, so current can only flow from the battery positive terminal to the switch. This side of the circuit has what is known as *potential voltage* – it's got 12 volts from the battery ready to use. On the other side of the switch, there are zero volts available. So there's a difference of 12 volts between the two sides of the switch. We call this the *voltage difference*.

Now close the switch: Current flows across the switch and the voltage difference vanishes. Voltage on either side of the

switch is equal. The switch has little or no resistance and there are 12 volts on either side. The circuit is complete; there is continuity and current flows from the source through the wires and the switch to the load, then back to the battery.

## Voltage drop

When the current passes through a load, the process is slightly different. A potential of 12 volts is applied to the positive side of the component, but this time it has to overcome a resistance to generate the required current flow. Because the resistance of the component is designed to provide just the number of amps needed by the component, the voltage is almost entirely used up in the process. We have a *voltage drop*.

We could say that the voltage is being used up as it pushes current across a resistance. It's important that you understand the concept of voltage drop because, practically speaking, it means that there's no voltage on the ground return side of the circuit. Voltage drop across the load is essentially equal to voltage supplied.

In the real world of real circuits, of course, things aren't quite as neat as the above description of voltage drop. There's a tiny voltage drop in the switches and feed wires of a circuit, so the load receives a fraction less than full source voltage. There's also a very small voltage drop in the earth return circuit, so that also affects the actual voltage drop across the load.

1654-1-1.5 HAYNES

*In this circuit, the switch is open, so there's a 12-volt potential on one side of the switch and no voltage on the other side*

*In a series circuit, current must pass through each load on its way back to the battery*

We'll show you how voltage potential and voltage drop can be applied in automotive electrical diagnosis and troubleshooting in Chapter 3. Now lets look at the three basic types of circuits – series, parallel and series/parallel – which you'll encounter in automotive electrical systems.

## Series circuit

A series circuit has two or more loads in sequence. Current has to pass through each load to complete its path back to the battery. A break at any point in the circuit, either on the feed side or the earth side, whether it's a break in the wire or a failure of a component, stops all current flow in the circuit.

A series circuit has the following important characteristics *(see illustration)*:

1 *Current (amperage) is the same everywhere in the circuit.*
2 *Voltage drop varies in proportion to the resistances.*
3 *Circuit resistance is the total of all the resistances in the circuit.*

The easiest way to understand these three characteristics of a series circuit is to visualise a bunch of water pipes forming a continuous loop. Now let's put a water pump in there somewhere to create current flow (the 'water pump' in an actual automotive electrical circuit is, of course, the battery). Okay. Start up the pump and what happens? The water starts circulating through the pipes. It just goes round and round, through the pipes, back to the pump, through the pump, back through the pipes, etc. If the pipes have the same internal diameter throughout the entire circuit, the flow rate of the water (amperage in an electrical circuit) is the same everywhere too. But the push delivered by the pump (voltage) diminishes as it gets farther from the pump. If the diameter of the pipes is the same throughout, the push from the pump diminishes at a constant rate. If some of the pipes have smaller diameters, the resistance to flow goes up in these areas and the push delivered by the pump (voltage) diminishes more quickly; if some of the pipes have larger diameters than the others, the push from the pump doesn't go down as much.

## Parallel circuit

The accompanying illustration shows a parallel circuit. Each

load in the circuit has a separate feed wire and a return path to earth. In a parallel circuit, current doesn't have to pass through all the components to complete the circuit; the circuit is completed through each one separately. A break in an individual earth wire, or a component failure, will not affect the operation of the other components.

A parallel circuit has the following important characteristics *(see illustration)*:

1 *Current at a branch of the circuit varies if the resistance of that branch's loads varies.*
2 *Voltage drop across all the loads is the same.*
3 *Circuit resistance is less than any single resistance.*

Now, let's look at our analogy again: Visualise a parallel circuit of water pipes with a pump circulating water through them. In this circuit, it's the water flow rate (current) – not the push (voltage) – that varies. Why? Think of one of those Y-splitters that allow you to attach two garden hoses to a single tap. Turn on the valve for one hose and turn off the valve for the other hose, then turn on the tap full blast; a healthy stream of water comes out of the hose that's attached to the On valve. Now open the valve for the other hose; water also comes out the second hose, but it's only half as strong in force as the stream from the first hose, and

*In a parallel circuit, each load has a separate feed wire – current doesn't have to pass through all the components to complete the circuit*

*In a series-parallel circuit, one load is in series with two or more other loads in parallel with each other*

1654-1-1.8 HAYNES

the stream from the first hose is itself only half what it was. The force, or push, from the water pressure in the line (voltage) is the same, but when you open the second valve, the total resistance goes down (because total hose area increases). Flow (amperage) through either of the two hoses

1654-1-1.9 HAYNES

*Opens are physical breaks anywhere in the circuit . . .*

*. . . and can occur in wires, as shown here, or at components*

is less than it would be through a single hose. The actual rate of flow through each hose depends on that hose's internal diameter (resistance). If both hoses have the same diameter, the current flow through each is the same; if one hose is bigger or smaller than the other, the current flow is proportionally bigger or smaller.

## Series-parallel circuit

The series-parallel circuit is a combination of the previous two types. In this type of circuit, one load is in series with two or more other loads, which are in parallel with each other.

A series-parallel circuit has two important characteristics *(see illustration)*:

1 *The voltage drop across the loads in parallel with each other will be the same.*
2 *The sum of the voltage drop at the first load and the drop across either of the other two loads equals the source voltage.*

When you're looking at wiring diagrams for your vehicle, you'll find circuits are often neither series nor parallel, but series-parallel. The trick is to figure out just what part of the circuit it is that you're checking (the series part or the parallel part).

## Circuit malfunctions

In Chapter 3 we'll familiarise you with electrical troubleshooting techniques. Here we'll discuss the three basic types of malfunctions that can occur in an electrical circuit.

### Opens

An open is a physical break anywhere in the circuit. It can occur in the wiring, at connections, or even within a component. When an open occurs, there is no longer any current flow, either because it's unable to, reach the load at all or can't return through the earth path to the source *(see illustrations)*.

*A short (indicated by the lightning bolt symbol in this drawing) causes current to find a new path to the source – in this example, the two motors (marked 'M') will operate even when the switch is open – when the switch is closed, the motors will slow down slightly and the light bulb (the load in series) will glow dimly*

*Shorts can occur between wires . . .*

## Shorts

Shorts occur when damage to wiring or a component causes a circuit to find a new path back to the source. In cars, shorts normally occur between two wires or between a wire (or component) and earth *(see illustrations)*.

In Chapter 3, we'll discuss how to read the symptoms of a short and locate it.

*. . . between a wire and earth/ground (as shown here) or even within a component*

## Excessive resistance

When there is excessive resistance in a wire or load, the load(s) try to draw the same current, which in turn causes a higher than normal voltage drop. If resistance increases enough, the effect can be the same as an open: No current at all gets through to the load.

Normally, excessive resistance causes components in the circuit to operate at reduced efficiency: lights are dim, electric motors run at slower than normal speed, etc.

The cause of this type of symptom is usually dirty or corroded contacts or terminals. Dirt or corrosion acts like insulation between two parts of the circuit *(see illustration)*. Another common cause is a chafed or partly broken wire, which reduces the available cross-sectional area through which current can flow.

## Switches

Automotive electrical circuits are almost always controlled by a switch of some sort. Switches do two things: Allow current into a circuit and direct the flow of current within a circuit.

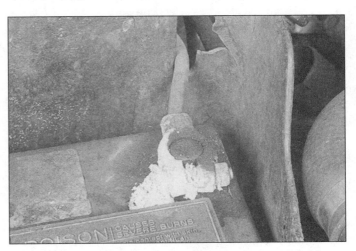

*Corrosion like this on a battery terminal can cause enough resistance to prevent the engine from starting – always check carefully for corrosion, loose connections and chafed or partly broken wires when you suspect excessive resistance in a circuit*

*The single-pole, single-throw (SPST) switch has only two positions – On and Off*

*Automotive switches are actuated in a variety of ways – top, left to right: toggle, rocker, push-pull knob, rotary knob, pushbutton and door jamb (actuated by the opening and closing of a door) – bottom: slide and pushbutton combination switch – this terminology tells you how to operate the switch, but it doesn't tell you how it functions electrically*

Switches come in a wide variety of configurations, and some look pretty complicated *(see illustration)*. But they all perform one, or both, of the above functions.

The following describes the types of switches (classified by electrical function) you are likely to find on your vehicle.

## Single-pole, single-throw switch

The single-pole, single-throw (SPST) switch is the simplest design *(see illustration)*. The 'throws' refer to the number of output circuits; the 'poles' refer to the number of circuits completed by the switch. The SPST has only two positions – On and Off. It either completes or 'breaks' the circuit. The reversing light switch on vehicles with a manual transmission is a typical example: Put the transmission in Reverse – the

switch closes the circuit to the reversing lights and they come on. Put the transmission back in Neutral or a forward gear – the switch opens and the lights go out.

The momentary contact switch is another type of SPST switch *(see illustration)*. A spring-loaded contact on this switch keeps it from completing the circuit until pressure is applied to the button. Because the spring holds the contacts open, this switch is sometimes designated as a normally open type. The horn switch is a good example of the normally open design. Another variation is the normally closed switch, which has closed contacts until the button is pressed.

## Single-pole, double-throw switch

The single-pole, double-throw (SPDT) switch has three terminals (one wire in and two wires out). One goes to the battery the other two go to separate circuits or loads *(see illustration)*. Either load can be connected to the battery, depending on the position of the switch. The high beam switch is an SPIDT switch. Some SPIDT switches are known as *centre-off* switches because they have three positions –

*On a momentary contact SPST switch, a spring-loaded contact keeps the switch from making contact until pressure is applied to the button*

*The singe-pole, double-throw (SPDT) switch has three terminals – one goes to the battery and the other two go to separate circuits or loads*

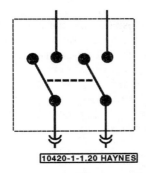

10420-1-1.20 HAYNES

*The double-pole, single-throw (DPST) switch has two positions (On and Off), but the switch actuator controls two circuits*

On, Off and On. They control one load in each of the On positions and break both circuits when the control actuator is in between.

## Double-pole, single-throw switch

The double-pole, single-throw DPST) switch has only two positions – On and Off. But, unlike the SPST switch, it has two independent poles, each connected to its own circuit *(see illustration)*. Each pole has two terminals. Think of the DPST as two SPST switches in one housing, with a common control actuator. The DPST can operate two separate loads at the same time. Headlight/running light switches are sometimes a DPST design.

## Double-pole, double-throw switch

The double-pole, double-throw (DPDT) switch has two independent poles, each with two On positions. Think of the

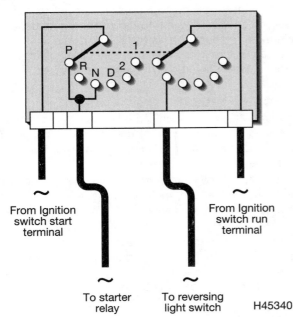

From Ignition switch start terminal

From Ignition switch run terminal

To starter relay

To reversing light switch

H45340

*This neutral start switch is an example of a multiple pole, multiple throw (MPMT) switch*

10420-1-1.21 HAYNES

*The double-pole, double-throw (DPDT) switch has a pair of poles, each with two On positions – think of the DPDT as two SPDT switches in one housing and operated by one actuator*

DPDT switch as two SPIDT switches in one housing, operated by one control actuator *(see illustration)*. The DPDT switch has six terminals: three for each pole.

## Single-pole, multiple-throw switch

The single-pole, multiple-throw (SPMT) switch allows you to select various settings for a device, such as a heater fan. This type of switch is usually wired to a series of resistors that control the current being fed to the device. Typical settings are Off, Low, Medium and High.

## Multiple-pole, multiple-throw switch

Switches can be designed with a large number of poles and throws *(see illustration)*. For instance, one type of starter inhibitor switch (allows you to start vehicles with an automatic transmission only in Neutral or Park) has two poles and six throws. It's referred to as a multiple-pole, multiple-throw (MPMT) switch. It has two movable wipers that move in unison across two sets of terminals (when you see a dotted line between the wipers on an MPMT symbol, it indicates that the wipers are mechanically linked).

## Rheostats

Have you ever wondered how the illumination intensity of the instrument panel is adjusted from dim to bright? It's a rheostat, also known as a variable resistor, that makes this possible *(see illustration)*.

Here's how a rheostat works: One end of a piece of coiled resistance wire is connected to the battery feed wire. The other end of the wire isn't attached to anything. The wire from the rheostat to the load is attached to a movable element called a *wiper*. The

*This rear view of a rheostat shows the coiled resistance wire used to vary the resistance in the switch*

*This Ford resistor assembly is typical of heater blower motor resistors – the coiled resistance wires are used to control blower motor speed*

*When current flows through a conductor, an electromagnetic field is produced around it – this field remains as long as the current continues to flow through the conductor*

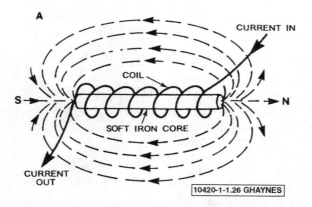

*If you wrap a conductor around an iron core, the field surrounding the wire will induce electromagnetism in the core – the more coils wrapped around the core, the greater the magnetism induced in the core*

wiper is mounted so it rubs against the resistance wire. When the wiper is close to a the battery-feed-wire-end of the resistance wire, the rheostat imposes little additional resistance to the circuit. But as you slide the wiper to the far end of the resistance wire, current flows through increasingly more resistance to get to the wiper, reducing current flow to the load. You can dial in any amount of resistance you want – from zero to high. This feature gives you precise control over the amount of current being fed to the load.

## Heater blower fan switches

Rheostats aren't usually capable of carrying high current without burning out. High current circuits which need variable resistance are usually equipped with a single-pole, multiple-throw slide switch. The typical three-speed blower switch for a heater is the most common example of this application. Fan motor speed is determined by the position of the switch. Depending on the switch position, the current is routed through different resistors in series with the motor *(see illustration)*. In the Low position, all the resistors are used. As the switch is turned to the next higher speed, a resistor is bypassed; as it's turned to the next speed, another resistor is bypassed, and so on. In the High position, all the resistors are bypassed, providing full current to the motor. Unlike the coiled resistance wire in a rheostat, these resistors are capable of taking higher current without damage (but they do get hot, so they're often located right in the blower air stream).

## Relays and solenoids

Relays switch current on and off in parts of the circuit where it would be inconvenient, or impossible, for you to do it yourself. Solenoids allow you to move mechanical devices from remote locations. Relays and solenoids are electromagnetic devices, so let's take a quick look at electromagnetism before we discuss these devices.

## Electromagnetism

When current flows through a conductor, an electromagnetic field around the conductor is produced *(see illustration)*. This field remains as long as the current continues to flow through the conductor.

If you wrap this conductor around an iron core and flow current through the wire, the electromagnetic field surrounding the wire will induce electromagnetism in the core *(see illustration)*.

As a general rule, the more times the wire is wrapped around the core, the greater the magnetism induced in the core. Again, the magnetism will remain in the core only as long as current flows through the wire.

## Relays

A relay is an electric switch that allows a small current to control a much larger one. It consists of an electromagnetic

*Cutaway of a typical relay*

*Cutaway of a typical solenoid*

coil, a fixed core and a movable armature *(see illustration)*. The armature, attracted by magnetism in the core, moves whenever the coil is energised. The relay has a control circuit (the small current which activates the relay) and a power circuit (the large current that is switched on or off by the relay). When the control-circuit switch is open, no current flows to the coil, so the coil has no magnetism. When the switch is closed, the coil is energized, making the soft iron core into an electromagnet, which draws the armature down. This closes the power circuit contacts, connecting power to the load(s).

When the control switch is opened, the current stops flowing in the coil, the electromagnetism disappears and the armature is released, breaking the power circuit contacts. Relays of this type are generally used only for short duration contact because of the high amount of current needed to energise the coil. For relays that remain in operation for longer periods, two windings are provided – one to pull the armature down and a second, lighter winding that breaks the circuit on the first winding and holds the relay in operation with much less current drain.

## Solenoids

Solenoids provide mechanical movement in areas on the vehicle where it is impossible, or inconvenient for you to reach. Solenoids are used to engage starter motors, lock and unlock doors and actuate engine and transmission control devices.

A solenoid consists of an electromagnetic coil surrounding a movable metal core, or plunger *(see illustration)*. When the coil is energised, the magnetic field pulls the core until it's centred in the coil. Usually, a return spring pulls the core back to its un-centred position when power to the coil is shut off. The movable core provides the mechanical movement. Solenoids are also sometimes used to close contacts, acting as a relay at the same time.

Solenoids that may remain in use for long periods of time are sometimes constructed with more than one winding – one heavy one to pull the core in, and one lighter one to hold it in. The heavier winding is usually called the *primary* or *pull-in* winding, while the lighter one is called the *secondary* or *hold-in* winding.

## Circuit protection

When an overload in a circuit cause too much current to flow, the wiring in the circuit heats up, the insulation melts and, sometimes, a fire starts – UNLESS the circuit has some kind of protective device. Fuses, fusible links and circuit breakers are designed into circuits to afford protection from overloads.

## Fuses

Fuses are the most common form of circuit protection used in cars. They're mounted either in a fuse panel or in-line *(see illustrations)*. Early designs use a strip of low melting-point metal enclosed in a

*Typical methods of installing in-line fuses*

*Fuse panels are often located under the driver's side of the dash panel – check the owner's manual for the location on your vehicle*

**Traditional fuse (good fuse on the top, blown fuse on the bottom)**

**Ceramic fuses are often used on European cars (good fuse on the left, blown fuse on the right)**

Bad        Good

**Modem miniature fuse (good fuse on the right, blown fuse on the left)**

10420-1-1.34 HAYNES

**Cutaway of a typical fusible link**
1 The link will burn through here     2 Small wire

glass tube or placed on a ceramic insulator *(see illustration)*. A newer 'miniature' type has spade connectors and is enclosed in a plastic housing *(see illustration)*. In operation, they both work exactly the same way: If an excessive current flows through the circuit, the fuse element melts at the narrow portion, opening the circuit and preventing damage.

Fuses are designed to carry a preset maximum current, and to 'blow" when that maximum is exceeded. The maximum current flow in amps is marked on the fuse. Always replace a blown fuse with a new fuse of the correct rating, both in type and current capacity.

Usually, a visual check of a fuse will suffice. Sometimes, however, a fuse can have an open in it even when it's not obviously blown. In Chapter 3, we'll show you how to check that kind of condition.

## Fusible links

While fuses protect individual circuits, fusible links are designed to protect the entire electrical system. Fusible links are short lengths of smaller gauge wire usually installed between the battery and the ignition switch, or between the battery and the fuse panel. Because they're a lighter gauge wire (and a different material) than the main conductor, they'll melt and open the circuit before damage can occur in the rest of the circuit *(see illustration)*. Fusible link wire is sometimes covered with a special insulation that bubbles when it overheats, indicating the link has melted. To replace a fusible link, you simply cut it out of the conductor or unbolt it and replace it with a new one. We'll show you how in Chapter 3.

## Circuit breakers

Circuit breakers are used in circuits where temporary overloads are not uncommon, and in circuits where power must be rapidly restored (headlights, windshield wipers, etc.). The typical circuit breaker is made of a set of contacts controlled by an arm made of two kinds of metals that expand at different rates *(see illustration)*. When too much current flows in the circuit, this *bi-metal arm* becomes overheated and opens the contacts – and the circuit – because of the uneven expansion of the two metals. When the

Internal
View

External
View

10420-1-1.35 HAYNES

**A typical self-resetting circuit breaker**
1 Contacts   2 Bi-metallic arm

**Manual reset circuit breaker**
1 Bi-metallic arm    2 Coil    3 Contacts

current stops flowing, the bimetal arm cools, once again closing the circuit. If the overload is still present, the circuit breaker once again 'cycles.' If the overload is gone, the circuit continues to function in a normal manner. This type of circuit breaker is known as a *cycling*, or *self-resetting* design because – after opening the circuit to protect it against overload – it automatically reconnects the circuit each time.

Another type of circuit breaker is referred to as non-cycling or manually resettable. In this type, there's a coil wrapped around the bimetal arm *(see illustration)*. When an over current exists and the contacts open, a small current passes through the coil. This current through the coil isn't large enough to operate the load, but it's sufficient to heat up both the coil and the bimetal arm. That keeps the arm in the open position until power is removed from the coil. On this type of circuit breaker, you'll see a button somewhere on the case or housing. To reset the breaker (shut off the power to the coil), you simply push in on the button.

## Multiplexing and networks

### Multiplexing

As vehicles become more and more complex, the amount, and weight of vehicle wiring harnesses become a significant factor in their design and construction. In order to reduce the amount of wiring, some later models are being equipped with Multiplex wiring.

Using this system, electrical actuators/motors/controllers are connected to a 'ring' loom of two, or three, wires. One wire supplies the electrical power, whist another is the vehicle ground (earth). The remaining wire is the 'signal' wire.

The central control unit sends a signal to the relevant component to operate. The processor within that component recognises the signal, and connects the component to the power and earth wires. On two wire systems, the signal from the control unit is embedded in the electrical power, in the form of a frequency modulation, or pattern.

### Networks

As the requirements relating to fuel economy, exhaust emissions, driving safety, in-car entertainment and comfort become ever more stringent, intensive communication between the various vehicle Electronic Control Units (ECUs) becomes necessary. To avoid the physical connections between these units becoming unmanageable (some ECUs had 121 connector pins), Bosch developed a system whereby all these components communicate via one or two wires. These wires are known as a 'data bus'. Each ECU has an integral transceiver which sends and receives data 'packets' along these wires *(see illustration)*. As the packet travels

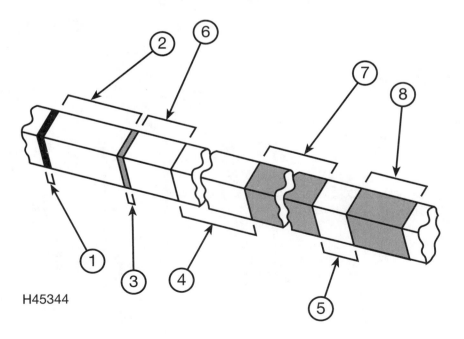

**Data 'packet' – CAN data bus**
1   Start field *(1 bit)*
2   Status field *(11 bits)*
3   Unused *(1 bit)*
4   Data field *(64 bits max.)*
5   Confirmation field *(2 bits)*
6   Check field *(6 bits)*
7   Safety field *(16 bits)*
8   End field *(7 bits)*

H45344

along the data bus, each ECU examines the packet and checks whether it needs the data or ignores it. Using this system allows rapid and reliable data transfer between the ECUs/controllers of a network. The first manufacturer to use this system in a production vehicle was VW. They named the system CAN (Controlled Area Network) Data Bus.

### CAN

This system consists of one or two wires connecting various ECUs within the vehicle. Each ECU is equipped with a transceiver for receiving and transmitting the data 'packets'. The first system had a data bus speed of 62.5 kbit/s (62,500 bits per second), but later speeds increased to 500 kbit/s. In areas of high electromagnetic interference and radiation emission (ie. the engine compartment), two wires are used in the network to provide an interference elimination system.

### LIN

Where speed of data transfer and interference is not a concern, some manufacturers use a single wire data transfer system known as LIN (Local Interconnect Network). Here the transfer rate is 1 to 20 kbit/s. Typical usages of this network are air conditioning controls, sun roof, heated windscreens, central locking, etc. The network is organised into one designated master control unit and up to 16 slave units, and works like this: The driver operates the sunroof switch, which places a data 'packet' requesting the sun roof to open, on the LIN. When this 'packet' is received by the master control unit (in this case, the air conditioning control unit), it places a 'packet' commanding the roof to open on the LIN. This 'packet' is recognised by the roof motor control unit which obeys the command. The major benefit of this system is security. Anyone attempting to 'hot-wire' a component of the system (eg. the door locks) would find it almost impossible to manipulate the component without being able to imitate the LIN master control unit signal characteristics including the unique identifier section of the signal 'packet'.

### Bluetooth

With the ever increasing use of mobile communication and information technology (mobile phones, PDAs, notebooks, etc.), traditional methods of exchanging information (hard-wire, infrared, etc.) are no longer suitable. Each component would have its own transfer protocol, and communication between units could be complex and unreliable. In order to standardise communications between mobile units, Bluetooth™ technology has been developed. A group of over 2000 companies from the fields of telecommunications, data processing, equipment and vehicle manufacturing cooperated and developed a standard for short distance (10 metres) radio signal transmission. This technology is being incorporated into motor vehicle design, and allows mobile devices to integrate with the vehicles networks (see illustration).

## Fault finding

Obviously from a fault finding perspective, the traditional probing with a multimeter may not reveal the expected results, and may cause damage. Fortunately, vehicles with Multiplex wiring and/or Networks are also equipped with sophisticated self-diagnosis systems, which monitor the integrity of circuits, controllers and components of the vehicle. Fault-finding using an appropriate reader/scanner should be relatively straight-forward and precise. However, as expensive ECUs and components are involved, always interrogate the system for stored faults first, and always examine the relevant wiring diagram before getting the multimeter out and backprobing connectors.

H45345

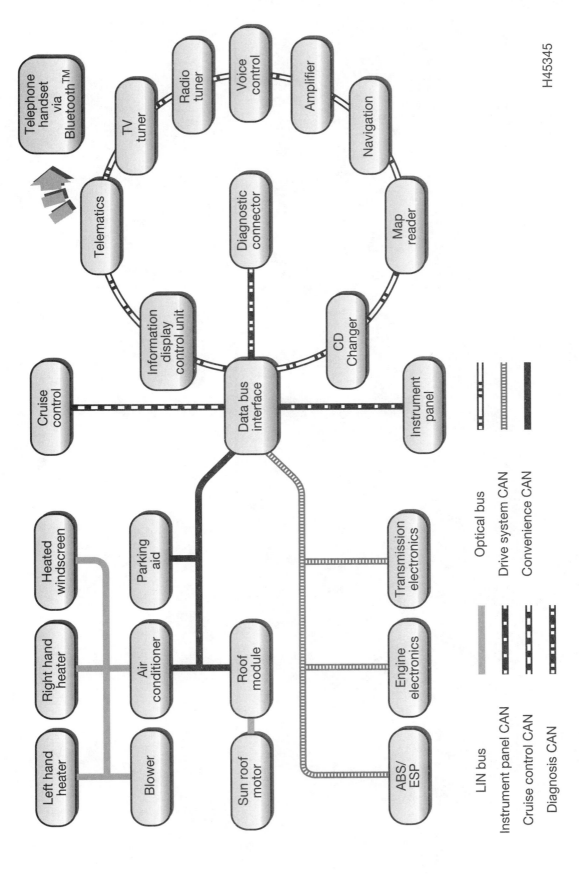

**Telephone handset via Bluetooth™**

**TV tuner**

**Radio tuner**

**Voice control**

**Amplifier**

**Navigation**

**Telematics**

**Diagnostic connector**

**Map reader**

**Information display control unit**

**CD Changer**

**Cruise control**

**Data bus interface**

**Instrument panel**

Optical bus

Drive system CAN

Convenience CAN

**Heated windscreen**

**Parking aid**

**Transmission electronics**

**Right hand heater**

**Air conditioner**

**Roof module**

**Engine electronics**

**Left hand heater**

**Blower**

**Sun roof motor**

**ABS/ESP**

LIN bus

Instrument panel CAN

Cruise control CAN

Diagnosis CAN

*Typical vehicle network layout*

# Notes

# *Understanding wiring diagrams*

General information

Components of a wiring diagram

Reading wiring diagrams

## General information

Wiring diagrams are very useful tools when troubleshooting electric circuits. Electrical systems on modern vehicles have become increasingly complex, making a correct diagnosis more difficult. If you take the time to fully understand wiring diagrams, you can take much of the guesswork out of electrical troubleshooting.

If you have an older vehicle, you may find the wiring diagrams difficult to decipher. Frequently, older diagrams give no information on component location, operation or how to read the diagram. Many of them are organized in ways that make tracing wires difficult.

Today's wiring diagrams tend to be more carefully organized, and the cross-references between each portion of the diagram are clearly explained. They often have component locators and some are even in colour (to show wire colours) *(see illustrations)*.

*Many modern diagrams like this one show individual circuits – this is a radio system circuit*

*A diagram from the early 1970s - many older diagrams have little information on where the components are located, how they work or how to read the diagram*

## Components of a wiring diagram

Wiring diagrams can be broken down into three main components: symbols, colour codes and wire gauge numbers.

### Symbols

On wiring diagrams, symbols are used to represent the components of the electrical system. The most obvious symbol is a line to represent a wire. Some other symbols are not so obvious, since they do not necessarily look like the components they're representing. That's because most wiring diagram symbols, which are sometimes called schematic symbols, show the way the component functions electrically rather than how it appears physically (see illustration).

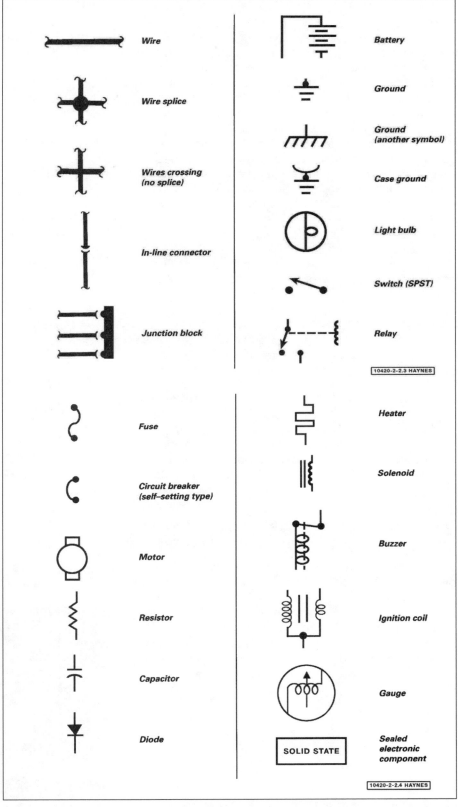

*Typical wiring diagram symbols - these symbols vary somewhat from manufacturer to manufacturer*

## Colour codes

Since wiring diagrams are usually in black-and-white, colour codes are used to indicate the colour of each wire. These codes are normally one or two-character abbreviations. These codes vary somewhat from manufacturer to manufacturer; however, most diagrams include a colour code chart so its easy to check the meaning of each code *(see illustration)*.

Occasionally, manufacturing difficulties cause a manufacturer to deviate slightly from the wiring colours shown on the diagram. If the wire colours at a connector do not match the diagram, and you're sure you're looking at the correct diagram, you can usually identify the incorrect colour by comparing all the colours at the connector with the diagram.

Wires are not always solid colours. Often they have markings on them such as a stripe, dots or hash marks. When a diagram shows two colours for a wire, the first colour is the basic colour of the wire. The second colour is the marking *(see illustrations)*.

## Reference numbers

Some manufacturers (notably Peugeot) do not colour code the wires. Instead they use a reference number system printed onto the outer insulating sleeve of the wire. This number should correspond to a the number printed alongside the wire on the wiring diagram *(see illustrations)*.

## Wire gauge numbers

The wire gauge number represents the wire thickness. (We'll tell you more about wire gauge in Chapter 3). In a wiring diagram, the gauge number for each wire is usually listed either before or after the colour code.

## Reading wiring diagrams

Wiring diagrams either show the entire electrical system on one page, or they split up the electrical system onto multiple pages and have cross-references which tie them all together. When a diagram is split up, there are usually charts with the diagram that explain the cross-referencing system.

The accompanying illustrations show examples of wiring diagrams from various manufacturers and the methods they use to cross-reference and show components *(see illustrations on pages 2•5 onwards)*.

| | | | |
|---|---|---|---|
| BK | Black | O | Orange |
| BR | Brown | PK | Pink |
| DB | Dark Blue | P | Purple |
| DG | Dark Green | R | Red |
| GY | Gray | T | Tan |
| LB | Light Blue | W | White |
| LG | Light Green | Y | Yellow |
| N | Natural | | |

*A typical colour code abbreviation chart*

*Examples of wire markings*

*This example code is for a green wire with a black stripe - the 1.25 is the metric wire gauge number*

*Peugeot use reference numbers printed on the wire insulation to identify their circuits*

**Peugeot wiring diagram**
*1 Component number*   *2 Connector socket number*   *3 Connector colour*   *4 Wire reference number*

*Typical key and matching wiring diagram from Haynes*

**Note:**
All **switches** and **contacts** are illustrated in the **mechanical off position.** The various contacts in a switch are shown in the current track to which they belong by function.

**Numbers in yellow squares** indicate that a wire is discontinued in the diagram and refer to the current track where it is continued.

**Wire cross section in mm²**

**Wiring colours** (are shown in the actual colours to be found on the vehicle)

**Numbers/number combinations**
These indicate the individual contacts in a multi-point connector, e.g. T 10/4
T 10 = ten-point connector
/4 = contact 4

**Terminals with the numbers which are on the actual parts.**

**Symbols** (in this case: bulb)

**Parts designation**
Using the legend you will be able to find which part in the current flow diagram is referred to by this symbol, e.g. W = interior light

**Internal connections** (thin lines)
These connections are not to be found in the form of wires. Internal connections are however current-carrying connections. They make it possible to check the flow of current within a component or unit.

**Numbers in circles** indicate the locations of earthing points (see legend)

**Current track numbers** to help you find the parts in the current flow diagram

*Typical wiring diagram from VW*

**1** This tells you the circuit is hot (receiving power) at all times
**2** This is a 20-amp fuse located in the fuse panel
**3** The BLK stands for a black wire
**4** This symbol shows the schematic details of a door lock switch assembly
**5** This symbol tells where the ground (earth) is located

*A typical Ford diagram (power door lock circuit shown)*

*A typical fuel and engine management system*

*A typical instrument cluster wiring diagram*

**Power distribution, starting and charging system**

*1 This is a 40-amp fusible link    2 This is a color code for a yellow wire with black stripe    3 This indicates a wire coming from another circuit*

# Notes

# Diagnosing and correcting circuit faults

## Introduction

The goal of any electrical diagnosis is to determine where the faulty component is located which prevents the current from flowing through the circuit as originally designed.

As manufacturers load up modern vehicles with electrical devices, the potential for problems increases dramatically. Due to the complexity of these electrical systems and the high cost of many replacement parts, a 'hit and miss' approach to troubleshooting is unsatisfactory. An organised and logical approach to diagnosis is essential to repair these electrical circuits in a prompt and cost effective manner.

Since electricity is invisible, specialised test equipment is necessary to trace circuits and check components. An accurate method of measuring electrical flow is essential if the problem is to be found without unnecessary parts replacement and wasted time.

In this Chapter we will show you how to select test equipment, how to operate it, how to troubleshoot electrical problems and how to make the connections necessary to repair wiring.

Troubleshooting procedures specific to starting systems, charging systems, lighting systems, gauge/indicator light circuits and power accessory circuits are located in Chapters 4, 5, 6, 7 and 8, respectively.

# Chapter 3

## Introduction to test equipment

### Jumper wires

Jumper wires are mainly used to find open circuits and excessive resistance by bypassing a portion of an existing circuit. They can also be used for testing components off the vehicle. They may be purchased already assembled or fabricated from parts purchased at an automotive accessory or electronics shop.

Jumper wires may be equipped with various types of terminals for different uses (see illustration). Jumper wires used to carry current from the battery to a component should have an in-line fuse installed to avoid an overload and should also have insulated boots over the terminals to prevent accidental grounding.

**Warning:** *Never use jumpers made of wire that is thinner (of lighter gauge) than the wiring in the circuit you are testing. Always use a fuse with the same (or lower) rating as the circuit had originally.*

### Test lights

Test lights are used to check for voltage in a circuit while power is connected to the circuit. Test lights are among the least expensive testing devices available and should be included in every tool box. They may be purchased already made-up or fabricated from parts purchased at an automotive or electronics supply store. Test lights come in several styles, but all have three parts in common; a light bulb, a test probe and a wire with a ground connector (see illustrations). Six, 12, or 24-volt systems may be tested by changing the bulb to the appropriate voltage. Although accurate voltage measurements aren't possible with a test light, large differences may be detected by the relative brightness of the glowing bulb.

**Note:** *Before using a test light for diagnosis, check it by connecting it to the battery, ensuring the bulb lights brightly.*

The very latest test lights look almost identical to the traditional ones, but have the wire and connector omitted. Instead, when the tester's hand is placed on the end of the tool, the LED lights if there is a voltage present.

*Jumper wires may be equipped with various types of terminals for different uses*

*A test light is a must for automotive electrical testing*

*The test light bulb may be changed to match the voltage of the vehicle being tested*

## Test buzzers

Test buzzers work the same way as test lights; however they offer the advantage of remote operation. For example, one person working alone may test the brake light circuit by stepping on the brake pedal and listening for the sound of the buzzer connected to the brake light bulb socket. A test buzzer may be fabricated at home from parts purchased at an electronics shop or made with jumper wires and a key reminder buzzer (see illustration).

Test buzzers are used in the same manner described for test lights. Additionally, they may be used to find shorts to ground/earth. The procedure for this is covered in the Section entitled Using test equipment.

*This test buzzer was made from a lights-on reminder buzzer salvaged from a breakers yard*

## Continuity testers

Continuity testers (also known as self-powered test lights) are used to check for open or short circuits. They consist of a light bulb, battery pack and two wires combined into one unit (see illustration). They may be purchased from an automotive accessory or electronics shops. Continuity testers must only be used on non-powered circuits; vehicle battery voltage would burn out the low-voltage tester bulb.

**(!)** *Caution: Never use a self-powered continuity tester on circuits that contain solid state components, since damage to these components may occur.*

*This continuity tester uses its own batteries to power the light bulb located in its tip*

## Short finders

Short finders are electromagnetic devices designed to trace short circuits quickly and easily. One part of the short finder is a pulse unit which is installed in place of the fuse for the circuit where a short is suspected. The other part of the short finder is a hand-held meter which is moved along the faulty wiring harness. Meter deflections indicate the area in the harness where the short is located. Short finders are available from major tool manufacturers (eg. Eastwood Co.) for a moderate price (see illustration). The savings from one use can often offset the purchase price.

*Short finders consist of a pulse unit and a separate hand-held meter*

## Analogue (gauge-type) multimeters

Analogue multimeters are suitable for a variety of test functions requiring the measurement of volts, ohms and amperes *(see illustration)*. Many brands and varieties are available at tool and electronics stores and by mail order. The units offering the most features and scales are usually the costliest. Analogue multimeters can't be used to test solid state circuits, such as computers and electronic ignition control modules. If you already have one of these units, by all means use it for performing the tests described in this book.

*Analogue multimeters can be used to measure volts, amps and ohms in non-solid state circuits*

## Digital multimeters

Digital multimeters are used for measuring volts, ohms and amperes with a high degree of accuracy *(see illustration)*. They are more readily available, more accurate and less expensive than analogue meters. Digital multimeters are compatible with solid state circuits, so you only need to buy one type of tester.

*Digital multimeters can be used for testing all types of circuits*

## Fault code readers

Modern cars (post 1998) are usually equipped with sophisticated self-diagnosis systems, which monitor some or all of the vehicle's electrical systems, identify any faults found, and store a fault code for later retrieval. Although these systems are primarily associated with diagnosing engine running faults etc. they may also record short- and open-circuits to many of the vehicle's components. Using a fault code reader to interrogate a vehicle's self-diagnosis system via the diagnostic plug, might save a lot of time *(see illustration)*. With the short- or open-circuit identified, tracing the fault with a multimeter should be straight forward.

*A fault code reader can be used on modern vehicles to extract stored fault codes via the diagnostic plug*

## Using test equipment

Before you can go chasing electrical gremlins, you have to know how to use test equipment. In this Section we will explain how to use the various testers introduced previously.

**Note:** *Most testers come with instructions. If they differ from the general procedures described here, follow the specific instructions provided by the manufacturer of the tester.*

**(!)** *Caution: Never connect solid state/electronic circuits to battery voltage and never test them with any device other than a digital multimeter.*

*Here a jumper wire is used to complete an earth circuit on a windscreen wiper motor*

### Checking for a bad earth/ground

Connect the jumper wire between the component case (or earth/ground terminal) and a clean bare metal spot on the vehicle chassis *(see illustration)*. If a circuit works properly with the jumper wire in place, but doesn't work when the jumper wire is removed, the earth/ground circuit has an open (or high resistance) which needs repair – check for loose connections, corrosion and broken component earth/ground straps.

### Checking the operation of a component designed to operate on full battery voltage

Earth/ground the component with a jumper wire as described above and connect a fused jumper wire from the positive battery terminal to the positive terminal on the component being tested *(see illustration)*. If it now works normally, remove the earth/ground jumper wire. If the device stops working, the earth/ground connection is definitely faulty, but the other side of the circuit may also be bad. Repair it. If the device continues working with the earth/ground jumper removed, look for an open in the positive side of the circuit. If the device won't work, even with both jumper wires in place, the component is faulty. Replace it.

*Components may be tested by connecting them directly to the battery with the jumper wires*

### Checking for voltage

**With a test light**

To use a test light, connect the earth/ground wire to a clean, bare metal earth/ground which is connected to the vehicle chassis. With the circuit switched on, insert the probe into the terminal or socket to be checked. If necessary, the probe can be pushed through the insulation to make contact with the wire *(see illustration)*. If the bulb lights, voltage is present, meaning the part of the circuit between the test light and the battery is free of open circuits. After testing is complete, tape over any wires punctured by the probe. Test lights are not sensitive to polarity and can be connected with either the probe or the earth/ground wire connected to positive or negative.

*The test light probe can be pushed through a wire's insulation – be sure to wrap electrical tape around the puncture after testing is complete*

**With a test buzzer**

Test buzzers may be connected and used the same way as test lights. Their main advantage is that they allow one person to perform tests which normally require an assistant. For directions on using test buzzers for finding shorts, see Tracing short circuits below.

**With a voltmeter**

Set the voltmeter scale selector switch to the appropriate range (this normally should be higher than battery voltage) and check to see if the test leads are connected to the correct terminals on the tester. The negative lead is black and the positive lead is red. When measuring the voltage in a portion of a circuit, the voltmeter must be connected in parallel with the portion of the circuit to be measured. To avoid damage to the meter, always connect the negative lead to the negative side of the circuit (earth/ground) and connect the positive lead to the positive side of the circuit (the power source side) *(see illustration)*.

*Be sure the test leads are connected properly – positive to positive and negative to negative*

## Checking for continuity

Continuity may be checked with a number of devices. If the circuit has power to it, a voltmeter, test light or test buzzer may be used as described above. If the circuit is not powered, an ohmmeter or self-powered continuity tester should be used.

 *Caution: Do not attempt to use a self-powered continuity tester or ohmmeter on a powered circuit. The test device will be damaged.*

To use a continuity tester, first isolate the circuit by disconnecting the battery or removing the fuse or circuit breaker. Select two points along the circuit through which there should be continuity *(see illustration)*. Connect one lead of the tester to each point. If there is continuity, the tester will light.

**Note:** *The procedure for checking continuity with an ohmmeter is similar to the procedure using a continuity tester. If there is continuity, the ohmmeter will read close to zero ohms (no or very low resistance). The procedure for checking resistance below points out some other special considerations when using an ohmmeter.*

*Here a wire and connector plug is being checked for continuity – if the bulb in the tester is lit, the circuit is complete*

## Checking resistance

Resistance is checked with an ohmmeter. An ohmmeter is normally one of the functions included in a digital or analogue meter. Turn the scale selector switch to the proper ohms range for the device you will be measuring. Make sure the wires are connected to the proper plugs on the meter and turn the meter on *(see illustration)*. Check that the meter reads 'infinity' before testing is begun, then touch the test probes together to ensure the meter goes to zero. Connect one test lead to the positive terminal of the device being tested and connect the other lead to the negative terminal or housing (earth/ground). After testing, switch the ohmmeter off to conserve the batteries.

*Using a digital multimeter to test the resistance of a speaker. The speaker resistance (impedance) is normally printed on the reverse of the casing*

## Tracing short-circuits

Short-circuits to earth/ground are most easily found with a short finder, although a test buzzer is also effective. If you use a buzzer and discover the short is not at a component (meaning it is somewhere in the wiring harness), inspect the exposed portions of the wiring harness for obvious evidence of a short (burned wire insulation, chafing, etc.). Check for where the wiring harness has to bend – eg. when the door or tailgate opens. If you still can't find the wiring harness short-circuit, we recommend you borrow or purchase a short finder. Finding a hidden short in a wiring harness without this device can be very time consuming.

**With a short finder**

1  *Remove the blown fuse, leaving the battery connected.*
2  *Connect the pulse unit of the short finder across the fuse terminals.*
3  *Close (turn on) all switches in series with the circuit you are troubleshooting.*
4  *Operate the short finder. The short finder will pulse current to the short. This creates a pulsing magnetic field surrounding the circuit wiring between the fuse panel and the short.*
5  *Beginning at the fuse panel, slowly move the short finder meter along the circuit wiring (see illustration). The meter will show current pulses through the sheet metal and body trim. As long as the meter is between the fuse block and the short, the needle will move with each current pulse.*
6  *When you have moved the meter past the point of the short, the needle will stop moving. Examine the wiring in that area for the short to ground and repair as needed.*

**Note:** *A test light or voltmeter may be substituted for the buzzer. However, an assistant will be needed to watch the light or meter while you disconnect components and wiggle the wiring harness.*

**With a test buzzer**

1  *Remove the blown fuse, leaving the battery connected.*
2  *Attach the alligator clips of the test buzzer to the fuse terminals.*
3  *Close (turn on) all the switches that are in series with the circuit you are troubleshooting.*
4  *If the circuit is still shorted to earth/ground, the buzzer will sound (see illustration).*
5  *Beginning at the load (the component that is operated by the circuit), disconnect each component in the circuit. Work your way backwards along the circuit until the buzzer stops sounding. Also, wiggle the wiring harness from side-to-side in areas where it's exposed.*
6  *When the buzzer stops, carefully check the portion of the circuit you just disconnected (or the part of the wiring harness you were wiggling) for a short. If disconnecting a switch, relay or harness connector caused the buzzer to stop sounding, the short is either at that component or somewhere between the component and the load.*
7  *Repair or replace components or wiring as needed.*

**The short finder pulse unit is connected to the fuse terminals in place of the fuse**

**A test buzzer may be used to find a short; connect it to the fuse terminals in place of the fuse**

# Chapter 3

## Checking voltage drop

This test checks for voltage being lost along a wire, or through a connection or switch while current is flowing.

  1  *Connect the positive lead of a voltmeter to the end of the wire (or to the side of the connection or switch) which is closer to the battery.*
  2  *Connect the negative lead of the voltmeter to the other end of the wire (or the other side of the connection or switch).*
  3  *Select the voltmeter range just above battery voltage.*
  4  *Switch on the circuit (see illustration).*
**Note:** *When no current is flowing, there can be no voltage drop.*
  5  *The voltmeter will show the difference in voltage between the two points. A difference (or drop) of more than about 0.2 to 0.3 volt indicates a problem (except when the voltmeter is connected across a load, in which case a substantial voltage drop is normal).*
  6  *Clean and repair the connections as needed or replace any faulty components.*
**Note:** *Ammeters are always connected in series with the circuit being tested (except units with inductive pickups).*

### Checking current flow with an ammeter

  1  *To connect an ammeter into a circuit, unplug a fuse or connector and attach the test leads to the exposed terminals. Remember, the ammeter must always be connected in series with the circuit (see illustration).*
  2  *Switch on the circuit and read the amperage shown on the meter. If it shows a negative reading, reverse the test lead connections. No reading at all indicates an open (incomplete) circuit.*
  3  *The reading should be less than (but not substantially less than) the circuit's fuse rating. If the reading is substantially less than the fuse rating, there's excessive resistance somewhere in the circuit. If the reading is higher than the fuse rating, there's a short to earth/ground.*

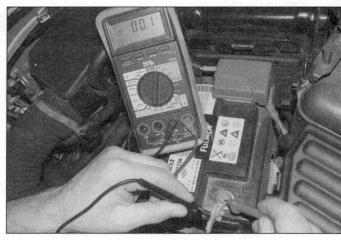

*Here a battery terminal is being checked for voltage drop – in this case, a drop greater than 0.1 volt means the terminal and clamp should definitely be cleaned!*

*Current flow (amperage) in a circuit may be checked by connecting an ammeter to the fuse terminals (with the fuse removed)*

## Testing relays

**Note 1:** *Chapter 1 covers the general operating principles of relays and the terminology of their parts. The information that follows does not apply to polarity-reversing relays, which are used in some power accessory circuits. See Chapter 8 for more information on these relays.*

**Note 2:** *Some circuits on some newer vehicles use solid-state (electronic) relays. This procedure applies only to electro-mechanical (non-electronic) relays. Electronic relays must be tested by a dealer service department or suitable equipped automotive electrical specialist.*

We strongly recommend using the correct wiring diagram for your vehicle to determine the proper connections for the relay you're testing *(see illustration).*

*The relays are often mounted on or near the fuse panel*

However, if wiring diagrams are not available, you may be able to determine the test connections from the information that follows.

## Relays with four terminals

On most relays with four terminals, two of the four terminals are for the relay's control circuit (they connect to the relay's coil). The other two are for the relay's power circuit (they connect to the armature contact and the fixed contact).

If you have wiring diagrams for the vehicle, you can figure out which terminals connect to which parts of the relay (see Chapter 2 for information on wiring diagrams). Often, relay terminals are marked as an aid.

As a general rule, the two thicker gauge wires connected to the relay are for the power circuit; the two thinner gauge wires are for the control circuit.

Remove the relay from the vehicle and check for continuity between the relay's power circuit terminals. There should be no continuity.

Connect a fused jumper wire between one of the two control circuit terminals and the positive battery terminal. Connect another jumper wire between the other control circuit terminal and earth/ground. When the connections are made, the relay should click. On some relays, polarity may be critical, so, if the relay doesn't click, try swapping the jumper wires on the control circuit terminals.

With the jumper wires connected, check for continuity between the power circuit terminals. Now there should be continuity.

If the relay fails any of the above tests, replace it.

## Relays with three terminals

If the relay has three terminals, it's a good idea to check the vehicle's wiring diagram to determine which terminals connect to which of the relay's components. Most three-terminal relays are either case-earthed or externally-earthed.

On a case-earthed relay, one side of the relay's control circuit grounds through the relay case, eliminating the need for the fourth terminal. This type of relay requires the case to be securely connected to a good chassis earth/ground. Check this type of relay the same way you would a four-terminal relay, noting that one of the control circuit's terminals is actually the relay case.

On an externally-earthed relay, one of the relay's terminals is connected to a positive power source. We'll call this the battery power terminal. Inside the relay, the battery power terminal is connected to one side of both the relay's power and control circuits. Another terminal is connected to the other side of the control circuit; the circuit is completed through a switch to earth/ground. The third terminal is connected to the other side of the power circuit; it's earthed/grounded at the circuit's load component. This type of three-terminal relay is sometimes a plug-in type with no connection between the case and earth/ground.

To check an externally-earthed relay, remove it from the vehicle and check for continuity between the relay's battery power terminal and its power circuit terminal. There should be no continuity.

Connect a fused jumper wire between the battery power terminal and the positive battery terminal. Connect another jumper wire between the relay's control circuit terminal and earth/ground. The relay should click.

With the jumper wires in place, connect a test light between the relay's power circuit terminal and earth/ground. The test light should light. If the relay fails any of these tests, replace it.

## General troubleshooting strategies

Before you begin troubleshooting a circuit, it is imperative that you formulate a plan of action. Check for simple problems first, such as blown fuses, corroded or loose connections, burned out bulbs or broken, frayed, chafed or burned wires – these are also the most common problems (see illustration).

The previous two Sections acquainted you with test equipment and the procedures for using it properly. Now let's take a look at some of the methods professionals use when tracking down problems.

Operate the problem circuit in all modes. Determine what components, if any, in the circuit still work. Is it a complete or partial failure? What other circuits are affected? When does it occur? Is the problem intermittent or does it happen all the time? Be sure to check the operation of all other electrical components on the vehicle. Sometimes what seems

*Check for simple things first, like corroded fuse connectors*

to be a problem affecting only one component is also causing (or being caused by) a problem in another circuit. If necessary, make notes of all the affected components and the specific symptoms. This will help you figure out the problem after you've looked at the wiring diagrams and had a chance to think about it. Think carefully about all the electrical components which have been disturbed or worked on recently. These are prime suspects.

## Problems affecting a single component

If a single component of a circuit is affected, start to test at that component and work back toward the fuse panel. Use a logical process of elimination to narrow down the problem. For example, if you find that only one side light is inoperative, you have eliminated the fuse, switch and main wiring harness as potential sources of the problem. Here are four conditions that cause single component failures and how to check for them:

### The component is not receiving current

With the circuit switched on, test for voltage at the component. If there's no voltage, continue to test for voltage in the circuit, working backward toward the fuse panel. When you reach a point where there is voltage, you know the problem lies between that point and your last test point.

### The component is not earthed/grounded properly

This condition can be tested two ways: 1) With power to the component, you can test for a voltage drop between the component and earth/ground. The drop should be less than 0.2 to 0.3 volt. 2) With power removed from the component, you can check for resistance between the component and earth/ground. The reading should be zero (or very close to zero) ohms.

### The component itself is faulty

For components designed to operate on full battery voltage, check the operation using a fused jumper wire, as described in the previous Section. For components that operate on less than battery voltage, measure the resistance or check for a voltage drop.

### The wiring is faulty

This can be checked two ways: 1) With no power to the circuit, check continuity. 2) With power to the circuit, check for a voltage drop in the wiring.

## Problems affecting multiple components

If the fault affects multiple components, start to test at the point where the circuit gets its power (usually the fuse panel or fusible link). Check the fuses, circuit breakers and/or fusible links (see Chapter 1, if necessary). If the circuit protection devices are blown, look for a short circuit; if they are intact, look for an open circuit or wires from different circuits contacting each other.

Obtain the wiring diagrams for the specific vehicle you are working on whenever possible.

Read about the various types of circuits described in Chapter 1 and learn how to tell which type you are working on.

Familiarize yourself with the current flow in the circuit by tracing the path in the wiring diagram (see Chapter 2). Determine where the circuit receives current, what the circuit protection is, what switches and/or relays control current flow and how the components operate.

Identify each component in the wiring diagram for the circuit you are testing and find the components on the vehicle.

Sometimes, multiple components can be affected by two wires from different circuits contacting each other. Take, for example, two simple circuits, each having one light bulb and an SPST switch. If the wires between each switch and each bulb come into contact with each other, closing either one of the switches will light both bulbs, but one or both bulbs will light more dimly than normal. Closing the other switch will alter the relative brightness of the two bulbs. In complicated circuits, there may be many symptoms, affecting several components, all related to such a problem.

## Intermittent problems

The most difficult type of electrical problem to diagnose is an intermittent one. Intermittent open circuits or short circuits are usually caused by something rubbing or a component that changes resistance when it heats up or cools down. Corroded and loose connections are also frequently the cause of such problems.

Note when the problem occurs and try to discover how to duplicate the problem during diagnosis. For example, if it only happens when you're going around a corner or over rough ground, wiggling the wiring harness may duplicate the problem. If it only happens after the engine is completely warmed up, heating the suspected faulty parts with an electric hair dryer may duplicate the problem. If the problem only occurs during wet weather conditions, a water misting bottle may help you duplicate the problem. Once you can duplicate the problem, follow the test procedures applicable, based on the symptoms.

## Make the repair

Once the diagnosis has been made, replace the faulty component or repair the wiring as necessary. After the repair has been made, operate the system and confirm that your repair has removed all the symptoms and has not caused any new problems.

## Type of connectors

### Electrical connections

Cars typically have many types of electrical connectors for different purposes (see illustration). With the increasing complexity of modern car electrical systems and the advent of computer control systems, many special connector types have made their appearance. Before we show you how to make your own electrical connections, let's take a look at the types of connectors commonly used on cars.

### Crimp connectors

To make their own electrical connections, many professional electrical technicians pick from the variety of crimp connectors available (see illustration). Crimp connectors are not as weatherproof as soldered connections, but, when you use a special tool, making these connections is quick and easy. If you choose the un-insulated variety of these connectors, you can ensure a weatherproof connection by soldering it after you make the crimp, then insulating it with heat shrink tubing. Later in this Section we'll show you how to make crimp connections, solder and use heat shrink tubing.

### Tubular butt connectors

Butt connectors may be used to join two stripped wire ends together permanently (see illustration).

### Ring terminals

Ring terminals go completely around a stud or screw (see illustration). They make good electrical and mechanical contact and don't come loose from terminal blocks easily.

### Hook and fork terminals

Hook/fork terminals are similar to ring terminals, but they have an open side (see illustration). Their advantage is they may be quickly connected to a terminal block. Their disadvantage is they come loose easier than ring-types. They're best suited to temporary installations.

*Many types of connectors are used on modern cars and trucks*

*Crimp connectors are available with and without insulation*

*Butt connectors are available in a variety of diameters to fit different wire gauges*

*Ring terminals are available for different wire gauges and stud sizes*

*Hook and fork terminals – from left-to-right; insulated fork terminal, insulated hook terminal, uninsulated hook terminal*

***Two types of bullet connectors***

***When used in pairs, the male and female ends of bullet connectors should be staggered like this to prevent incorrect connections***

***Male and female ends of flat blade connectors***

***Two brands of snap-splice connectors showing top and bottom view***

## Bullet connectors

Bullet connectors are available in male and female types *(see illustration)*. When used in pairs, they may be installed with male and female ends on adjacent wires to prevent improper connections *(see illustration)*. Bullet terminals are generally used for components that are occasionally disconnected.

## Blade connectors

Also known as quick disconnect or push-on connectors, they are used on many fuse panels and accessories *(see illustration)*. They are also generally used for components that are occasionally disconnected.

## Snap-splice (Scotchlok) connectors

These connectors are frequently supplied with tow bar wiring kits and other accessory kits *(see illustration)*. The main advantage with this type of connection is that you don't have to cut the original wire to make a connection. However, they are not as reliable as soldered connections and have a low current capacity. To make a connection, place the two wires to be connected into position in the 'V' grooves in the metal portion of the connector. Close the flap, clamp the unit together with pliers and you are done.

## Multi-wire connectors

These connectors are made to connect two or more wires simultaneously and are designed so they can only be installed one way *(see illustration)*. This protects you from reconnecting it improperly after you've disconnected it. Multi-wire connectors that were installed on the vehicle at the factory are available through a dealer parts department; aftermarket type connectors may be found in car accessory and electronics shops.

## Special connectors

Many types of special electrical connectors are used on modern computerised cars. Replacements for most of them are available from a car dealer/car accessory shop or check on the internet (eg. www.vehicle-wiring-products.co.uk).

***This is one half of multi-wire connector – the notched corner allows the terminal to be connected only one way; other designs of multi-wire connectors have tabs and slots on the connector housings for the same purpose***

*Depress the terminal locking tang with a small pick tool*

*The wire and terminal should slip out the back of the connector plug*

Prior to starting any repairs, obtain the necessary parts to complete the repair.

On many of these special connectors, it's possible to remove a single terminal from the connector so you can replace a component or repair a wire. To do so, separate the connector halves and remove any terminal covers or retainers. Depress the terminal locking tang using a small pick *(see illustration)*. Place the pick between the locking tang of the terminal and the plastic of the connector body and ease the wire back enough to release the locking tang. Gently pull the wire out the back of the connector plug *(see illustration)*.

Inspect the condition of the terminal and lead. If they are reusable, bend the tang back into shape with the pick. If the terminal needs replacement, attach a new one using the procedures described later in this Section under *Installing crimp connectors*.

Before inserting the lead, make certain that the terminal is shaped correctly. Gently insert the lead from the back of the connector plug. The terminal should stop or 'catch' about halfway into the connector body. Push back and forth gently on the lead to be sure the terminal is secure in both directions. Apply silicone grease to the terminal end to prevent corrosion and install the connector.

## Making connections

Now that you're familiar with the types of connectors available, we'll show you how you can make your own connections to repair the electrical system or add accessories.

### Stripping wires

Unless you're using snap-splice connectors (discussed earlier), the first step to making a connection is stripping the insulation off the wire(s) where the connection will be made.

If you are unsure of the wire size, begin with an opening in your wire stripper/crimper that barely cuts into the insulation and work down in size until the wire strips clean *(see illustrations)*. If

*Wire stripper tools are available at most tool shops, car accessory shops and electronics stores – many, like the ones shown here, can also be used to install crimp connectors – be sure to buy a good quality tool*

*Find the size opening that cuts the insulation but not the wire*

you intend to solder the wires together, strip about 12 mm (1/2-inch) of insulation off. If you are using crimp-type butt connectors, cut off just enough insulation (about 6 mm or 1/4-inch) so the wire will fill one side of the connector. Don't nick or cut any of the strands. Inspect the stripped end for nicks and cuts *(see illustration)*. If the wire is damaged, cut off the stripped end and repeat the process. Twist the strands about one-half turn to keep them together *(see illustration)*.

## Splicing wires

Wires enclosed in a harness must be separated to expose the individual wire during repair. If the harness is in a plastic conduit that has a lengthwise slit, simply slip the wire out. If the harness is taped, carefully cut and unwind the tape until the damaged portion of the wiring is exposed.

Cut the ends of the wire off cleanly, removing as little wire as possible. Strip the wire ends as described above.

**Note:** *If more than one adjacent wire is being spliced, stagger (or offset) the splices to avoid a thick lump in the harness (see illustration).*

At this point, you must choose between the various methods of joining wires. Most splices are made with crimp-type butt connectors. The insulated type should be used. If the splice will be exposed to the weather, the preferred method is soldering. Soldered joints can be insulated with heat shrink tubing or tape. The heat shrink tubing is recommended because it is more permanent and secure. Refer to the specific procedures in this Section for further information.

## Installing crimp connectors

Crimp connectors are available in a number of sizes which correspond to the wire gauge/thickness. The popular sizes use colour-coded insulation to make identification easier:

Red for 0.65 to 1.5 mm²

Blue for 1.5 to 2.5 mm²

Yellow for 3.0 to 6.0 mm²

If you're installing ring connectors, you must also select the proper stud size. These are commonly 3.2, 4.3, 5.3, 6.4, 8.4, 10.5 and 13 mm.

**⊘** *Caution: Always use insulated connectors on the positive side of the circuit. Most connectors are designed to be used with copper wire; to avoid dissimilar metal corrosion, use connectors that are compatible with the wire being used.*

**Be sure the strands of wire aren't damaged when the insulation comes off**

**Twist the strands to keep them together**

**Stagger the splices to avoid a thick lump in the harness**

**Strip away only enough insulation to fit the wire through the connector (usually about 6 mm or 1/4-inch)**

**Insert the stripped wire end(s) into the connector . . .**

**. . . then crimp the terminal securely onto the wire**

**This butt connector has been securely crimped onto the wires – note the indentations left by the tool**

Select the proper size and type of connector to be installed. Strip the insulation from the wire for a distance equal to the length of the connector barrel (usually about 6.0 mm or 1/4-inch) *(see illustration)*.

Slip the connector onto the wire. Position the crimping tool on the spot to be crimped. Squeeze the handles of the crimping tool together until the terminal barrel is fully crimped to the wire without excessive distortion *(see illustrations)*. Check the security of the crimp by pulling on the terminal.

## Soldering

Before you can begin, you will need a soldering iron or gun and solder *(see illustration)*. For automotive electrical systems, a soldering gun of 100/140 watts capacity is very handy. Soldering irons are less expensive but take longer to heat up. If you buy one, get it with about a 50 watt rating.

**Soldering guns and irons are available from the tool shops, car parts/accessory shops and electronic stores in a variety of brands and ratings**

**Keep the heat shrink tubing away from the heat while soldering**

**Twist the ends of the wires together . . .**

Solder is sold with various proportions of tin alloyed into it, most commonly 40/60, 50/50 and 60/40, with the percentage of tin listed first. 60/40 works well for wiring. Always use a resin core solder or soldering flux (Zinc and ammonium chlorides in petroleum grease – eg. Fluxite). This cleans the joint, removing oxides and other materials that would prevent a good connection.

**!** Caution: *Never use acid core solder or acid flux on electrical connections.*

If you intend to insulate the joint(s) with heat shrink tubing, slip one piece over each wire and push it back far enough to avoid any heat from soldering *(see illustration)*. Twist the ends of the wires you intend to join together *(see illustrations)*.

Practice on wire scraps before attempting actual repairs. Hold the soldering gun or iron against the wiring joint (underneath it).

**Note:** *Use a thick piece of wood as a work surface – don't use metal; it will conduct heat away.*

Once the wires are heated sufficiently, touch the solder to the wiring (not the soldering gun/iron tip) and allow the solder to flow into the wiring joint *(see illustration)*. If the solder balls up around the gun/iron tip and doesn't flow into the joint, the joint isn't hot enough; continue heating the joint. Remove the gun/iron and allow the solder to cool without disturbing the joint. When the solder cools, inspect the joint. The solder should have penetrated throughout the entire joint. Re-solder if necessary. Slip the heat shrink tubing into place (if used) and heat it as described under Insulating connections. If heat shrink tubing isn't available, apply tape to the joint for insulation.

**. . . until the splice looks like this**

**Heat the wire first, then add the solder**

*After connection are made, place the heat shrink tubing over the joints and heat it with a lighter or match*

*Wind the tape around the splice . . .*

## Insulating connections

Soldered and non-insulated crimp connections made on the positive side of the circuit must be insulated. Heat shrink tubing is the best way to insulate, since it does not unwind and come off over time like tape. Tape, however, is an effective insulation and can be used when shrink tubing is not available.

### Heat shrink tubing

Heat shrink tubing is available from electronics and car accessory stores. The tubing comes in various lengths and diameters. Select a diameter and length that will slip over the thickest part of the area to be insulated, overlapping the ends by about 6.0 mm (1/4-inch). To install heat shrink tubing, cut a piece to the appropriate length for each connection and slip it over each of the wires before the connection is made. After the connection is made, slide the tubing into position and heat it with a hot air gun or match/lighter until it shrinks around the wire *(see illustration).*

 *Caution: Don't hold the match/lighter too close or you will melt the tubing!*

### Tape

Electrical tape is available in a variety of materials and widths. For most purposes, quality 19 mm wide PVC tape with adhesive designed to remain sticky at low temperatures is best. Self-amalgamating tape is also available. Useful for waterproofing the connection, when the tape is wrapped over itself, it amalgamates to form a complete waterproof seal.

Centre and roll the tape over the entire splice. Roll on enough tape to duplicate the thickness of the original insulation. Don't flag the end of the tape *(see illustrations).*

*. . . overlapping both ends of the wire insulation*

If the wire isn't protected by a conduit or other harness covering, tape the wire again. Use a winding motion to cover and overlap the first piece of tape.

*Don't leave the tape with a flagged end like this*

*Fusible links are usually located near the battery*

## Replacing fusible links

Fusible links are normally replaced by obtaining a replacement from the dealer spares dept. Often the link is screwed into place *(see illustration)*.

For more information on fusible links, see Chapter 1.

## Choosing Wire

Sometimes, repairing the electrical system will involve replacing a section of wire. Since wire is by far the most common part of any electrical system, it's essential that you know a few things about selecting the right wire for the job.

Nearly all wiring in automobiles is constructed from stranded copper.

**(!)** *Caution: A few vehicles have some aluminium wiring; do not splice aluminium wires to copper – the dissimilar metals will corrode, causing electrical failure.*

Wire is specified by gauge/thickness, number of strands and type of insulation. Refer to the following information before you select wire.

### Wire gauge/thickness

The amount of current that a circuit can carry is dependent on the cross-sectional area, or 'gauge,' of the wire. Gauge represents the cross-sectional area of the wire itself (the conductor), NOT including the insulation.

In most automotive wire, over 60 percent of the total cross sectional area is insulation *(see illustration)*. If you don't want an electrical fire (from excessive resistance caused by a conductor that's too small), make sure you select wire based on the gauge of the conductor.

Manufacturers may refer to wire sizes on schematics in either American Wire Gauge (AWG) or Metric sizes. See the accompanying AWG Conversion Table for equivalency comparisons *(see illustration)*.

American Wire Gauge (AWG) sizes may be determined by measuring the diameter of the conductor (the bare wire) with the insulation removed. Refer to the Wire Gauge Diameter Table for dimensions.

When choosing wire gauge, the distance the wire must run and the amperage it will be expected to carry must be determined first. Refer to the Wire Gauge Selection Table. Note that you can always use thicker wire (lower gauge number) than is recommended.

### Number of strands

The term 'stranded' refers to the practice of using a number of smaller diameter wires instead of one larger one. Automotive electrical wire is stranded because of its flexibility and resistance to fracture. Stranded wire is 25 to 1200 times less likely to fracture than single-core wiring when exposed to vibration.

When referring to the number of strands, stranding is generally categorised as coarse, medium and fine. A battery cable is a typical example of coarse stranding. Under-the-dash wiring is medium strand. And constantly flexed wires, like those between the door and the body, or between the trunk and the body, are finely stranded.

Sometimes, the identifying number for a piece of wire will include the number of strands in the wire. Don't confuse this number with the wire gauge number!

### Wire insulation

As long as you buy quality name-brand wire, you don't have to worry too much about insulation. Most quality automotive wiring is insulated with corrosion and temperature-resistant synthetic materials such as polyvinyl chloride (PVC). However, you should know that PVC has its limits: It will soften when exposed to temperatures over 93° C (200° F) and change shape under its own weight. Eventually, it may distort enough to expose the conductor.

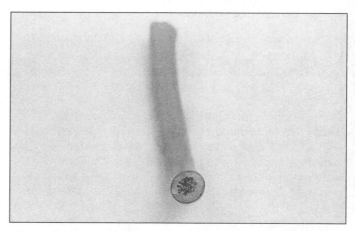

*About 60 percent of the total cross sectional area of this wire is insulation – gauge refers to the cross-sectional area of the conductor*

| Metric Size mm² | AWG Size |
|---|---|
| 0.5 | 20 |
| 0.8 | 18 |
| 1.0 | 16 |
| 2.0 | 14 |
| 3.0 | 12 |
| 5.0 | 10 |
| 8.0 | 8 |
| 13.0 | 6 |
| 19.0 | 4 |
| 32.0 | 2 |
| 52.0 | 0 |

| American Wire Gauge | Wire Diameter in inches |
|---|---|
| 20 | 0.03196118 |
| 18 | 0.040303 |
| 16 | 0.0508214 |
| 14 | 0.064084 |
| 12 | 0.08080810 |
| 10 | 0.10189 |
| 8 | 0.128496 |
| 6 | 0.16202 |
| 5 | 0.18194 |
| 4 | 0.20431 |
| 3 | 0.22942 |
| 2 | 0.25763 |
| 1 | 0.2893 |
| 0 | 0.32486 |
| 00 | 0.3648 |

| Circuit Amperes | | Circuit Watts | | Wire Gauge (for length in feet) | | | | | | |
|---|---|---|---|---|---|---|---|---|---|---|
| 6V | 12V | 6V | 12V | 3' | 5' | 7' | 10' | 15' | 20' | 25' |
| 0 to 2.5 | 0 to 5 | 12 | 24 | 18 | 18 | 18 | 18 | 18 | 18 | 18 |
| 3.0 | 6 | 18 | 36 | 18 | 18 | 18 | 18 | 18 | 18 | 16 |
| 3.5 | 7 | | | 18 | 18 | 18 | 18 | 18 | 18 | 16 |
| 4.0 | 8 | 24 | 48 | 18 | 18 | 18 | 18 | 18 | 16 | 16 |
| 5.0 | 10 | 30 | 60 | 18 | 18 | 18 | 18 | 16 | 16 | 16 |
| 5.5 | 11 | | | 18 | 18 | 18 | 18 | 16 | 16 | 14 |
| 6.0 | 12 | 36 | 72 | 18 | 18 | 18 | 18 | 16 | 16 | 14 |
| 7.5 | 15 | | | 18 | 18 | 18 | 18 | 14 | 14 | 12 |
| 9.0 | 18 | 54 | 108 | 18 | 18 | 16 | 16 | 14 | 14 | 12 |
| 10 | 20 | 60 | 120 | 18 | 18 | 16 | 16 | 14 | 12 | 10 |
| 11 | 22 | 66 | 132 | 18 | 18 | 16 | 16 | 12 | 12 | 10 |
| 12 | 24 | 72 | 144 | 18 | 18 | 16 | 16 | 12 | 12 | 10 |
| 15 | 30 | | | 18 | 16 | 16 | 14 | 10 | 10 | 10 |
| 20 | 40 | | | 18 | 16 | 14 | 12 | 10 | 10 | 8 |
| 25 | 50 | | | 16 | 14 | 12 | 12 | 10 | 10 | 8 |
| 50 | 100 | | | 12 | 12 | 10 | 10 | 6 | 6 | 4 |
| 75 | 150 | | | 10 | 10 | 8 | 8 | 4 | 4 | 2 |
| 100 | 200 | | | 10 | 8 | 8 | 6 | 4 | 4 | 2 |

**Wire gauge selection table**
*Find the amperage or watts the circuit is expected to carry on the left and the distance the wiring must run at the top – follow the columns until they intersect – for example, a 12 volt circuit which is 15 feet long and carries 10 amperes should use at least 16 gauge wire (1 foot = 30.5 cm)*

# Notes

# Starting systems

## Introduction

The starting system rotates the engine's crankshaft at a speed fast enough to start the engine. Through a circuit of heavy cables, connectors and switches, current from the battery travels to the starter motor, which rotates the crankshaft and, when everything is working properly, starts the engine *(see illustration)*.

In this Chapter, we will look at the starting system and its individual components, discussing operation, troubleshooting and repair.

### Starting system components
The typical starting system includes the following components:

*Starter motor*
*Battery*
*Cables and wires*
*Ignition switch*
*Starter solenoid (either on the starter or remotely mounted)*
*Neutral start switch (most vehicles with automatic transmissions)*
*Clutch interlock switch (some vehicles with manual transmissions)*

SOLENOID CONNECTS
BATTERY TO STARTER
MOTOR

STARTER
MOTOR TURNS

ENGINE CRANKS
OVER

10420-4-4.01 GHAYNES

*The electric starter system*

## Starter motor

The starter motor is a powerful electric motor which rotates the engine's crankshaft quickly enough (about 200 rpm) to start it. When the starter is energised, the starter's pinion gear meshes with the teeth on the flywheel (or driveplate) ring gear. The pinion rotates, which spins the flywheel (and thus the crankshaft) and starts the engine.

The starter motor has no method of cooling. It's intended to be operated for only short periods of time. If the starter isn't allowed to rest every 10 seconds or so – and given at least two minutes to cool off – the high current running through it can damage it in as little as 60 seconds.

## Battery

The battery supplies the electrical current that the starter needs to start the engine. The starter places a heavy load on the battery during starting, so the battery must have a strong charge.

## Cable and wires

Because the starter motor draws high current, heavy cable is used between the battery and the starter motor. Lighter gauge wires are used to control the solenoid.

## Ignition switch

The ignition switch closes the circuit that energises the starter solenoid.

The switch is normally mounted on the steering column and actuated by the ignition key.. When the ignition key is turned to Start, electrical voltage is sent to the starter solenoid from the battery.

## Starter solenoid

Nearly all modern vehicles use a solenoid mounted on the starter. This type of solenoid serves two purposes: 1) to connect the battery to the starter and 2) to bring the starter drive pinion into contact with the flywheel ring gear during starter operation – this type of starter is known as a pre-engaged starter. The solenoid consists of two windings mounted around a cylinder containing a moveable plunger. A shift fork is connected to the plunger, and a pushrod and contact disc are assembled in line with the plunger. When the windings are energised (by turning the ignition key to Start), the plunger moves, pulling the shift fork and

moving the drive pinion into mesh with the flywheel ring gear. The contact disc is pushed into firm contact with the two high-current terminals on the solenoid, connecting the battery to the motor.

The two windings in the solenoid are called the hold-in winding and the pull-in winding. The hold-in winding has fine wire windings and the pull-in winding has windings with a larger diameter wire. The pull-in winding and hold-in windings are used to pull the solenoid into position. Once the solenoid is in position, the magnetism from the hold-in winding is sufficient to hold the solenoid in position. The pull-in winding is shut off, permitting greater current flow through the starter motor. The pull-in winding is shut off when the contact disc contacts the high-current terminals.

## Neutral start switch

Vehicles equipped with automatic transmissions require a means of preventing the engine from being started while in gear. For this reason, most manufacturers include a neutral start switch which is operated by the shift linkage and ensures the engine will start only when in Park or Neutral.

## Clutch interlock switch

On some vehicles with manual transmissions, a starter/clutch interlock switch assures the vehicle will not start unless the clutch pedal is pressed all the way to the floor. This switch is mounted on the clutch pedal.

*A cutaway of a typical starter motor*

A  Drive gear housing
B  Solenoid plunger
C  Solenoid return
    spring
D  Solenoid
E  End frame
    insulator
F  Commutator end
    frame
G  Retainer
H  Clutch and drive
    assembly
I  Armature

**Exploded view of a typical starter motor and solenoid assembly**

## Starter motor design

To understand the design and operation of the starter motor, you need to recall some of the principles of electromagnets:

• A magnetic field is generated when current flows through a conductor.

• This field surrounds the conductor and extends over its entire length.

• The strength of this field is directly proportional to the amount of current flowing through the conductor.

• If the conductor is looped and placed within a second magnetic field, the two fields will interact. On one side of the loop, the fields will reinforce each other; on the other side, they will oppose each other.

The operation of all starter motors is based on these principles. Keep them in mind as you look at the following starter motor components (see illustrations).

### Armature

The armature is made of a soft iron core wrapped with many loops or 'windings' of insulated copper wire. The windings are mounted lengthwise on the core, which strengthens and concentrates the magnetic field produced by the windings when they're energised. The armature is mounted on a shaft and the ends of each winding are connected to the commutator segments. The commutator conducts current to the windings through the brushes (see illustration).

### Field coils

The field coils create a magnetic field that surrounds the armature and causes the armature to rotate. The field coils

**A typical armature and shaft assembly**

Field windings

Pole shoe

H45342

*A typical field coil*

are very strong electromagnets composed of heavy copper ribbons wound around soft iron cores called pole shoes. Each field coil is formed into an arc, so there is very little clearance between the coils and the armature rotating inside the coils *(see illustration)*.

## Brushes

The brushes supply electricity to the armature through the commutator. The brushes are mounted on the commutator end housing and lightly held against the commutator by springs.

## Drive assembly

The drive assembly is installed on the end of the armature shaft. When the starter is operating, the pinion gear rotates with the armature to crank the engine.

To prevent damage to the pinion gear when the engine starts and the flywheel is rotating faster than the starter, most modern vehicles use a roller-type overrunning clutch *(see illustration)*. This device transmits torque in only one direction, turning freely in the other. Thus, the pinion can be driven by the flywheel for the brief period so you have time to turn the key away from the Start position.

## Frame

The starter frame supports the armature, field coils and end housings. It also serves as a convenient earth/ground.

## Starter motor operation

When the ignition key is turned to the Start position, the starter solenoid is actuated. The solenoid allows current to flow to the starter motor.

Current flows through the armature and field coils. The electromagnetic force created between the armature and the field coils causes the armature to rotate. As the armature rotates, the pinion gear on the end of the drive assembly turns the flywheel ring gear. This causes the crankshaft to rotate.

## Batteries

The battery is a central component in the starting system. Its primary function is to supply the necessary current to operate the starter motor. When cared for properly, a battery can provide many years of satisfactory service. If neglected or abused, a battery can fail very quickly.

### Some miscellaneous battery facts

- *When left standing and unused, a battery loses about one percent of its charge per day.*
- *In winter, when heavy demand is placed upon the battery, it's a good idea to charge it occasionally. Discharged batteries freeze more easily than fully charged ones.*
- *A fully charged battery freezes at -65° C (-85° F), half-charged at -26°C (-15° F) and one-quarter charged at -9°C (+15° F).*
- *A fully charged battery at -17° C (0° F) has only 40 percent of the cranking power it has at 26° C (80° F).*
- *A battery left in a state of discharge will lose capacity.*

MESHING SPRING  CLUTCH HOUSING  SHELL  ROLLER SPRING

ROLLER

PINION GEAR

10420-4-4.10 GHAYNES

*A typical overrunning clutch assembly*

# Battery types

### 'Wet' batteries

These are the traditional lead/acid batteries *(see illustration)*. Usually a black box, containing positive and negative grids separated into 6 cells, and immersed in a solution of sulphuric acid. Hydrogen gas is produced as the battery is charged and discharged – this gas is either vented to atmosphere (traditional batteries) or condensed and drained and passed back into the cells (maintenance free batteries).

The cells grids are made of lead but a hardening agent is added to make the casting process easier. This might be antimony or, for maintenance-free batteries, calcium. Antimony will promote electrolyte gassing and loss of electrolyte, and calcium is being used in its place where minimal gassing is essential.

### Gel batteries

These are very similar in principle to wet batteries, but with the addition of silicic acid, the electrolyte is solidified into a gel-like mass *(see illustration)*. The advantage of this is a substantial increase in the charge/discharge cycle capacity – offering more favourable conditions for recharging after a deep discharge, which, in turn gives the battery a longer storage life. Other advantages include better protection against leaks, and a low build up of gas. The disadvantages are higher cost, less availability, not compatible with high temperatures (not for engine bay fitment) and poorer cold starting properties.

In contrast to wet batteries, the gel batteries are not vented directly to atmosphere, nor are the cells interconnected for gas discharge. Batteries not vented to atmosphere are classed as VRLA (Valve Regulated Lead Acid Battery). Instead the gasses produced during high loading are converted back into water in each respective cell. There is

1  Cover
2  Post
3  Electrolyte level mark
4  Intercell connector
5  Vent plug
6  Plate strap
7  Battery case
8  Bottom rail
9  Positive and negative plates
10 Plastic separators

©BOSCH

*Design of a Bosch battery*

however, a safety valve built into each cell to allow surplus gas (produced when over-charging) to escape. Since there is no provision for replenishing the electrolyte in these batteries, once gas escapes, the life of the battery could be seriously shortened.

### AGM (Absorbent Glass Mat) batteries

Here the electrolyte is solidified by absorbent glass mat *(see illustration)*. The glass mat is comprised of very fine interwoven glass fibres, and looks like a fleece. As the glass mat is highly absorbent the full volume of the electrolyte is absorbed, offering good protection against leaks as in the

H45347

**Gel type battery**

1  Gas vent channel
2  Cover plug
3  Solidified electrolyte (Gel)
4  Battery casing

H45346

**AGM (Absorbent Glass Mat) battery**

1  Gas vent channel
2  Electrolyte absorbed by glass mat
3  Battery case

event of the battery casing being damaged, the amount of electrolyte lost is negligible.

Like Gel batteries, AGM batteries are not vented to atmosphere, and are classed as VRLA. They too have a high capacity for charge/discharge cycles, but have enhanced cold starting properties. However, the disadvantages are high cost, low availability, and are not compatible with high temperatures so cannot be fitted into the engine bay.

## Battery warnings and precautions

Battery handling and servicing involves two hazardous substances: sulphuric acid and hydrogen gas.

### Sulphuric acid warnings

- *Sulphuric acid is the active ingredient in battery electrolyte (the fluid inside the battery). It's a powerful acid that will corrode all common metals, destroy paint finishes and clothing and inflict serious burns when it contacts skin and eyes.*
- *If you spill electrolyte on your skin, rinse it off immediately with water.*
- *If you get electrolyte in your eyes, flush them with water for 15 minutes and get prompt medical attention.*
- *If you accidentally ingest electrolyte, immediately drink large amounts of water or milk. Follow with milk of magnesia, beaten eggs or vegetable oil. Call a doctor immediately.*

### Hydrogen gas warnings

- *Most batteries give off hydrogen gas constantly. During charging, they give off even more. Hydrogen gas is highly explosive.*
- *When you service, charge or jump start a battery, make sure the area is well ventilated.*
- *Never allow flames, cigarettes or any device that might cause a spark anywhere near a battery being charged or jump started.*
- *When inspecting or servicing the battery, always turn the engine and all accessories off.*
- *Never break a live circuit at the battery terminals. An arc could occur when the battery, charger or jumper cables are disconnected, igniting the hydrogen gas.*

### Miscellaneous warnings and precautions

- *Always wear safety goggles when performing any work on the battery.*
- *When loosening cables or working near a battery, keep metallic tools away from the battery terminals. The resulting short circuit or spark could damage the battery or ignite the hydrogen gas around the battery.*
- *Always disconnect the battery negative cable first and connect it last.*
- *Never move a battery with the vent caps removed. Electrolyte can easily splash out.*
- *Always use a battery carrier when lifting a battery with a plastic case or place your hands at the bottom and end of the battery. If you're not careful, too much pressure on the ends can cause acid to spew through the vent caps.*
- *Use wing covers to protect the vehicle from acid spillage.*
- *Keep sharp objects out of the battery tray to avoid puncturing the case, and don't overtighten the battery retaining clamp.*

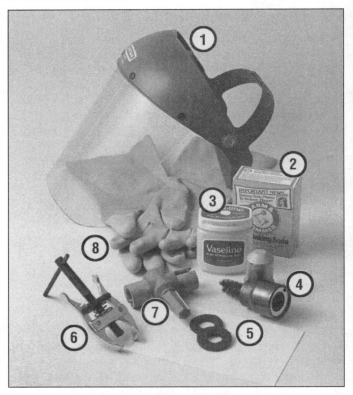

*Tools and materials required for battery maintenance*

1   Face shield/safety goggles – When removing corrosion with a brush, the acidic particles can easily fly up into your eyes
2   Baking soda – A solution of baking soda and water can be used to neutralise corrosion
3   Petroleum jelly – A layer of this on the battery posts will help prevent corrosion
4   Battery post/cable cleaner – This wire brush cleaning tool will remove all traces of corrosion from the battery posts and cable clamps. If you have a side terminal battery, you'll need one that is designed differently than this
5   Treated felt washers – Placing one of these on each post, directly under the cable clamps, will help prevent corrosion
6   Puller – Sometimes the cable clamps are very difficult to pull off the posts, even after the nut/bolt has been completely loosened. This tool pulls the clamp straight up and off the post without damage
7   Battery post/cable cleaner – Here is another cleaning tool which is a slightly different version of Number 4 above, but it does the same thing
8   Rubber gloves – Another safety item to consider when servicing the battery; remember that's acid inside the battery!

## Disconnecting the battery

Several systems fitted to modern vehicles require battery power to be available at all times, either to ensure their continued operation (such as the clock) or to maintain control unit memories (such as that in the engine management system's ECU) which would be wiped if the battery were to be disconnected. Whenever the battery is to be disconnected, first note the following, to ensure that there are no unforeseen consequences of this action:

a) *First, on any vehicle with central locking, it is a wise precaution to remove the key from the ignition, and to keep it with you, so that it does not get locked in if the central locking should engage accidentally when the battery is reconnected.*

b) *The engine management system's ECU may lose the information stored in its memory when the battery is disconnected. This includes idling and operating values, and any fault codes detected. Whenever the battery is disconnected, the information relating to idle speed control and other operating values may have to be re-programmed into the unit's memory. The ECU does this by itself, but until then, there may be surging, hesitation, erratic idle and a generally inferior level of performance. To allow the ECU to relearn these values, start the engine and run it as close to idle speed as possible until it reaches its normal operating temperature, then run it for approximately two minutes at 1200 rpm. Next, drive the vehicle as far as necessary – approximately 5 miles of varied driving conditions is usually sufficient – to complete the relearning process.*

c) *If the battery is disconnected while the alarm system is armed or activated, the alarm will remain in the same state when the battery is reconnected. The same applies to the engine immobiliser system (where fitted).*

d) *If a trip computer is in use, any information stored in memory will be lost.*

e) *If an audio unit is fitted, and the unit and/or the battery is disconnected, the unit may not function again on reconnection until the correct security code is entered. Details of this procedure, which varies according to the unit and model year, are given in the Owners Handbook supplied with the vehicle when new. Ensure you have the correct code before you disconnect the battery..*

Devices known as 'memory-savers' (or 'code-savers') can be used to avoid some of the above problems. Precise details vary according to the device used. Typically, it is plugged into the cigarette lighter, and is connected by its own wires to a spare battery; the vehicle's own battery is then disconnected from the electrical system, leaving the 'memory-saver' to pass sufficient current to maintain audio unit security codes and ECU memory values, and also to run permanently-live circuits such as the clock, all the while isolating the battery in the event of a short-circuit occurring while work is carried out.

> **(!)** *Warning: Some of these devices allow a considerable amount of current to pass, which can mean that many of the vehicle's systems are still operational when the main battery is disconnected. If a 'memory-saver' is used, ensure that the circuit concerned is actually 'dead' before carrying out any work on it.*

## Maintaining the battery

**Note:** *Several tools are required for battery maintenance. Refer to the accompanying illustration before undertaking the following recommended service procedures (see illustration).*

If you give a battery reasonable attention and care, its service life will be significantly longer than it will be if you don't. Proper maintenance also reduces the possibility of being stranded somewhere because of a dead battery.

Check the battery electrolyte weekly. Perform the other maintenance items listed below every three months or 3000 miles.

### Check the electrolyte

**Note:** *This procedure is only possible on batteries with removable caps. Many modern batteries have sealed tops that do not allow you to check the electrolyte level or add water; however, there's often an indicator in the top of the battery that gives an indication of its electrolyte level, as well as its state of charge. If you have a maintenance free battery with removable caps, it's a good idea to occasionally check the electrolyte level, regardless of the manufacturer's recommendations.*

Remove the vent caps on the battery. Look at the electrolyte solution and smell it. If it's in good shape, it should be clear. Discoloration and/or the presence of an odor similar to rotten eggs could indicate an excessively high charging rate (see Chapter 5) or an aged battery approaching the end of its service life.

Check the electrolyte level in each battery cell. It must be above the plates. There's usually a split-ring indicator in each cell to indicate the correct level. If the level is low, add distilled water only, then reinstall the caps.

> **(!)** *Caution: Overfilling the cells may cause electrolyte to spill over during periods of heavy charging, causing corrosion and damage to nearby components.*

If you have to add water frequently to the battery, inspect the case for cracks. If you can't find any cracks, the battery is probably being overcharged – check the charging system (see Chapter 5).

### Clean the battery

Clean the top and sides of the battery with a clean rag. Remove all dirt and moisture. Keeping the battery clean inhibits corrosion and also exposes cracks in the case, buckling and similar damage that might otherwise be hidden under the dirt.

Corrosion on the carrier, battery case and surrounding areas can be removed with a solution of water and baking

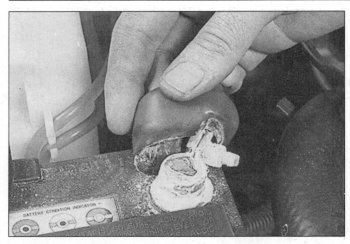

*Battery terminal corrosion usually appears as light, fluffy powder*

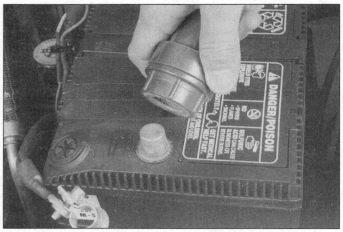

*Regardless of the type of tool used on the battery posts, a clean, shiny surface should be the result*

*When cleaning the cable clamps, all corrosion must be removed (the inside of the clamp is tapered to match the taper on the post, so don't remove too much material)*

soda. Apply the mixture with a small brush, let it work, then rinse it off with plenty of clean water *(see illustrations)*.

## Inspect the case and cover

Inspect the case for cracks or buckling. The presence of either of these symptoms could indicate any of the following conditions:

  a) *Over-tightened retaining clamp*
  b) *Slackened retaining clamp*
  c) *An excessively high charging rate causing the battery temperature to be too high (see Chapter 5)*
  d) *The battery has sat for a long time in an under-charged condition (buckled plates)*
  e) *Frozen electrolyte*

Look for acid deposits on the battery cover. These normally indicate overfilling or gassing and spewing from an excessively high charging rate (see Chapter 5).

Inspect the battery terminals for distortion, missing mounting bolts and corrosion. If corrosion is evident, disconnect the cables from the terminals, clean them with a battery brush and reinstall them. To minimize further corrosion, apply a layer of petroleum jelly to the terminals after you've reinstalled the cables.

Make sure the battery tray is in good condition and the retaining clamp is tight. If you remove the battery, make sure that nothing is in the bottom of the tray when you reinstall the battery. Don't overtighten the retaining clamp fasteners.

## Check the battery cables

Poor battery cable connections can cause starting problems and poor operation of the electrical system. The high current requirement of the starting system means that voltage loss through the cables must be minimised. Inspect the entire length of each battery cable for damage.

Look for cracked or burned insulation, frayed wire strands and corrosion. If you find any damage other than light corrosion, replace the cables – don't attempt to repair them.

If light corrosion is evident on either cable, detach it from the terminal and clean it with a wire brush. If the corrosion can't be completely removed, it's too far advanced. Replace the cable.

Don't forget to check the (often overlooked) engine-to-body earth-strap *(see illustration)*. If allowed to corrode or loosen, it can cause components earthing at the engine to malfunction.

*A typical engine-to-body earth strap*

# Replace any damaged or corroded cables

**Note:** *It's a good idea to replace battery cables in pairs, even if only one is visibly damaged.*

Detach the old cable from the battery.

After you have disconnected the old cable from the battery, trace it to its opposite end and detach it from the starter solenoid or earth location. Note the routing of each cable to ensure correct installation.

Take the old cables with you when buying new ones. It is vitally important that you replace the cables with identical parts. Just because a cable has the same length and post type does not mean it's a good replacement. Make sure you get a cable that has the same (or larger) wire gauge diameter as the original.

Clean the threads of the solenoid or earth connection with a wire brush to remove rust and corrosion. Apply a light coat of petroleum jelly to the threads to prevent future corrosion.

Attach the cable to the solenoid or earth connection and tighten the mounting nut/bolt securely, then reattach the cable(s) to the battery.

# Testing the battery

Before you begin testing the battery, perform all the checks listed under *Maintaining the battery* above. Often, you can identify the problem from these checks.

Nearly all battery manufacturers affix a battery date code to their batteries *(see illustration)*. Always refer to the battery's date of manufacture before proceeding with any tests. This information may help you decide if a battery is at the end of its service life.

The following tests will allow you to determine the battery's condition and also will help you find problems with the vehicle's electrical system that cause a constant drain on the battery.

### State-of-charge test

A battery cannot be accurately tested until it is at or near its fully charged state. Before proceeding to any other tests, check the state of charge using one of the methods described below. If the battery is not at the minimum charge level stated in the procedure below you're following, charge it. If the battery still won't reach the minimum level, replace it.

There are two common methods of checking the battery's state of charge: the hydrometer test and the open circuit voltage test. The hydrometer test has the added advantage of also revealing some types of internal battery damage. However, the hydrometer test can only be performed on batteries with removable caps.

### Hydrometer test (batteries with removable caps only)

This test allows you to check the state of charge of each of the battery's cells. It requires a hydrometer: a tool commonly available from car parts/accessory shops.

The hydrometer is a bulb-type syringe which, when squeezed and released, draws electrolyte from a battery cell *(see illustration)*. A float with a graduated specific gravity

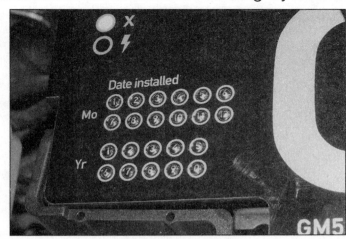

*Batteries are often marked with the first charge or installation date*

scale is housed inside the barrel of the hydrometer. When electrolyte is drawn in, the float rises and the specific gravity is read where the float scale intersects the level of the electrolyte in the hydrometer.

Specific gravity varies with temperature. As temperature rises, specific gravity decreases and vice versa. If the battery temperature is not 26° C (80° F), the reading must be adjusted.

**Note:** *If the vehicle has not been driven for several hours, the battery temperature should be the same as the outside air temperature.*

Remove all vent caps.

Make sure the electrolyte level is high enough to withdraw the proper amount of electrolyte into the hydrometer barrel. If it isn't, top up each cell with distilled water.

*Here's a battery hydrometer being used to draw electrolyte from a battery cell – this hydrometer has a thermometer on it so it's easier to make temperature corrections*

*To test the open circuit voltage of the battery, simply touch the black probe of a voltmeter to the negative terminal and the red probe to the positive terminal – a fully charged battery should read 12.6 volts or higher*

If the electrolyte level is high enough, you may proceed. If it isn't – and you have to add water – you'll have to wait a few hours before going on. Never take a reading immediately after you have added water. The water must mix thoroughly with the electrolyte for the hydrometer reading to be accurate.

Holding the hydrometer upright, squeeze the bulb tightly with your thumb and index finger and insert the hydrometer pick-up tube into the first cell.

Slowly release thumb pressure until the bulb is fully expanded and the float is suspended freely in the barrel (but not enough to force the float against the upper end of the hydrometer). Always hold the barrel vertically to prevent the float from binding or sticking to the sides.

With the hydrometer at eye level, read the float scale at the electrolyte level.

Squirt the electrolyte solution back into the cell.

*Battery load tester in use*

Record the specific gravity reading. If the battery temperature is not 26°C (80° F), correct the reading. For every 6 degrees above 26° C (80° F), add 0.04 to the specific gravity. For every 6 degrees below, subtract 0.04.

To determine the approximate battery charge indicated by the hydrometer reading, refer to the instructions that came with the hydrometer. If the reading is below 1.235, the battery must be re-charged before proceeding to any other tests.

Repeat for each cell in the battery. If the readings among the cells vary more than 0.050, the battery is internally damaged. Replace it.

When you're finished, disassemble the hydrometer in accordance with the manufacturer's instructions and rinse the barrel and float assembly with clean water. While the hydrometer is disassembled, inspect the float assembly for leaks. If the hydrometer can't be disassembled, suck clean water into it and expel it several times.

### Open circuit voltage test

This test requires a digital voltmeter.

The battery's surface charge must be removed before accurate voltage measurements can be made. Turn on the main beams for ten seconds, turn them off, then let the vehicle stand for two minutes.

With the engine and all accessories off, disconnect the battery's negative cable. Touch the negative probe of a voltmeter to the negative battery terminal and the positive probe to the positive terminal *(see illustration)*.

Read the voltage. A 12-volt battery at or near full charge for this test should read 12.6 volts or above. If it's less than 12.4 volts, charge the battery before proceeding with any other tests.

**Note:** *If the voltmeter reading is negative, you have connected the meter backwards. Swap the probes to the opposite terminals.*

### Battery load test

This test evaluates the battery's ability to operate the starter and other heavy electrical loads. It requires a special load tester. These testers are available in different designs from automotive tool and equipment suppliers *(see illustration)*.

All load testers draw current from the battery while measuring its voltage level. The voltage level of a good battery will remain relatively steady under load, but a defective battery will show a rapid loss in voltage. Battery cold cranking amperage and temperature will affect the test results, so follow the instructions carefully.

**Note:** *The following instructions should apply to most batteries and most testers, but always follow the instructions included with your tester if they differ from the following.*

Turn off the engine, vehicle accessories and the tester.

Attach the tester's positive clamp (usually red) to the positive battery terminal and the negative clamp (usually black) to the negative battery terminal.

With the clamps connected, the tester's voltmeter will

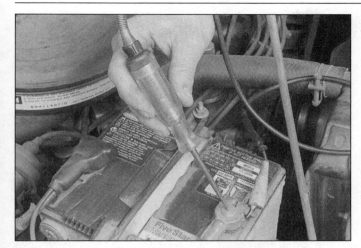

*To find out whether there's a drain on the battery, simply detach the negative cable and connect a test light between the cable clamp and the negative battery post – if the light comes on with all accessories off, there's a drain*

indicate the battery's state of charge. If the state of charge is less than 12.4 volts for a 12-volt battery, the battery must be recharged before load testing. If recharging doesn't bring the voltage up to 12.4 volts or more, the battery is defective. Replace it.

If the tester does not have an ammeter and has a load switch (not a dial), turn on the load switch.

If the tester is equipped with an ammeter, turn on the ammeter and rotate the load control knob to increase the load until the amperage reading is one-half of the battery's cold cranking amp (CCA) rating (listed on the battery). If the CCA rating is not listed on the battery, use the following guidelines to estimate battery size: Small (four-cylinder) engine – 300 CCA; medium (six-cylinder engine) – 400 CCA; large (8-cylinder engine) – 500 CCA. After the load is dialed in, switch the tester back to the voltmeter reading.

Maintain the load for 15 seconds. On 12-volt systems, the voltage reading should remain above 9.6 volts. The reading may be slightly lower if the outside air temperature is less than 21° C (70° F). Compensate meter readings in accordance with the following chart:

### Approximate temperature

| (degrees Celsius) | Minimum voltage |
| --- | --- |
| 21 | 9.6 |
| 15 | 9.5 |
| 10 | 9.4 |
| 5 | 9.3 |
| -1 | 9.1 |
| -7 | 8.9 |
| -12 | 8.7 |
| -17 | 8.5 |

If the voltage is below the minimum, replace the battery.

### Battery drain test

This test will indicate whether there's a constant drain in the vehicle's electrical system that can cause the battery to discharge.

Make sure no accessories are turned on. If the vehicle has an under-bonnet light, verify it's working properly, then disconnect it.

Detach the cable from the negative battery terminal and attach one lead of a test light to the cable end. Touch the other lead to the negative battery terminal *(see illustration)*. The test light should not glow. **Note:** *Refer to the information concerning battery disconnection given previously in this Section.*

If the light glows, it indicates a constant drain which could cause a discharged battery.

**Note:** *On vehicles equipped with on-board computers, digital clocks, digital radios, power seats with memory and/or other components which normally cause a key-off battery drain, it's normal for the test light to glow dimly. If you suspect the drain is excessive, connect an ammeter in place of the test light. The reading should not exceed 0.5 amps.*

The prime suspects for current drain problems are lights (under-bonnet, glove box, luggage compartment, etc.) that don't turn off properly. If the drain isn't caused by a light, remove the fuses one at a time until the cause of the drain is located. When you pull the fuse for the circuit that is draining the battery, the test light will go out.

If the drain is still undetermined, the problem is likely a shorted starter solenoid or a short in the wiring to the solenoid. Inspect the wiring and connections. If no short is found, disconnect the wires from the solenoid until the light goes out.

## Booster battery (jump) starting

 *Warning: Never attempt to jump start a frozen battery. It may explode.*

**Note:** *The cable connections for jump starting often allow only limited current flow. Depending on how much the battery's discharged, jumper connections may or may not start a vehicle with a weak battery.*

To avoid damage to the vehicle, the battery and yourself, observe the following precautions when using a booster battery to start a vehicle:

Position the vehicles so that the jumper cables will reach. But, MAKE SURE THE VEHICLES DON'T TOUCH EACH OTHER!

Make sure the transmission is in Neutral (manual) or Park (automatic).

Make sure the ignition switch is in the Off position.

Turn off the lights and other electrical loads.

# Chapter 4

**Note:** *If the vehicle you want to start is equipped with a computer, it's a good idea to turn on the heater blower motor. This will prevent damage to the computer in case of an excessive electrical surge.*

Make sure the booster battery is the same voltage as the discharged one in the vehicle.

Your eyes must be shielded. It's a good idea to wear safety goggles.

If the booster battery has removable vent caps, remove the caps and lay a cloth over the vent holes.

Make the jumper cable connections EXACTLY as follows:

a) Connect one end of the red jumper cable to the positive terminal of the discharged battery and the opposite end to the positive terminal of the booster battery.

b) Connect the black jumper cable to the negative terminal of the booster battery and then to a bolt or bracket on the engine block – NOT to the negative battery terminal – of the vehicle being jump started. This is an important precaution to prevent sparks which may cause an explosion. **Note:** *Some modern vehicles are equipped with an earthing point under the bonnet specifically for the negative jumper cable to connect to – check in the vehicles Owners Handbook supplied with the car (see illustration).*

Check the cables – make sure that they're not going to be in the way of the fan, drivebelts or any other moving parts when the vehicles are started.

Start the engine of the vehicle with the good battery and run it at a moderate speed.

Start the engine of the vehicle with the discharged battery.

Reduce the engine speed to idle on both vehicles and leave all switches off to prevent damage to the vehicle electrical systems.

Remove the cables in the reverse order they were attached.

## Charging a battery

> ⓘ *Warning: Charging batteries produce hydrogen gas, which is explosive. Charge batteries only in well ventilated areas and don't smoke or allow open flames or sparks anywhere near the battery. Always turn off the battery charger before connecting it or disconnecting it from the battery. Never attempt to charge a frozen battery. It might explode. Allow it to warm to 10° C (50° F) before connecting the charger.*

> ⓘ *Caution: If the vehicle is equipped with a computer, only trickle-charge the battery to ensure the computer is not damaged. If a charger with a high charge rate is to be used, disconnect the battery first.*

When the battery's state of charge has been depleted, it must be recharged. Charging is simply passing a current through the battery from positive to negative, instead of from negative to positive as in discharging. The charging process reverses the chemical action and restores the electrolyte to its original state before discharge.

Charging methods and types of chargers vary widely. Regardless of the method and equipment you use, charging must be done carefully to achieve proper results and avoid damage to batteries and possible personal injury. Chargers includes their own instructions. Always follow these instructions to the letter. Never disregard the safeguards and procedures provided by the manufacturer.

There are three basic charging methods – slow charging, fast charging and constant potential charging. Slow charging is a low current (about 2 to 5 amps) applied over a long period of time. Fast charging is a high current (about 15 to 35 amps) applied over a relatively short period of time. Constant potential charging uses a type of charger that varies the amperage based on the battery's state of charge (a high amperage at the beginning of the charge cycle that tapers off as the battery approaches full charge).

Generally, slow charging is best, since there is little chance of damaging the battery by overcharging (one of the major causes of battery failure). If you care about your battery,

**Make the booster battery cable connections in the numerical order shown (note that the negative cable of the booster battery is NOT attached to the negative terminal of the dead battery)**

| Reserve Capacity Rating | | 80 or Less | | | 81 - 125 | | | 126 - 180 | | | 181 - 250 | | | Above 250 | | |
|---|---|---|---|---|---|---|---|---|---|---|---|---|---|---|---|---|
| Charging Rate (Amperes) | | 5 | 10 | 20 | 5 | 10 | 20 | 5 | 10 | 20 | 5 | 10 | 20 | 5 | 10 | 20 |
| Open Circuit Voltage | Specific Gravity | Charging Time in Hours | | | | | | | | | | | | | | |
| 12.25-12.40 | 1.200-1.225 | 4 | 2 | 1 | 6 | 3 | 1.5 | 8 | 4 | 2 | 10 | 5 | 2.5 | 14 | 7 | 3 |
| 12.05-12.24 | 1.170-1.200 | 6 | 3 | 1.5 | 8 | 4 | 2 | 12 | 6 | 3 | 16 | 8 | 4 | 22 | 11 | 5 |
| 11.90-12.04 | 1.145-1.170 | 8 | 4 | 2 | 12 | 6 | 3 | 16 | 8 | 4 | 22 | 11 | 5.5 | 30 | 15 | 7 |
| Less than 11.90 | Less than 1.145 | 10 | 5 | 2.5 | 14 | 7 | 3.5 | 20 | 10 | 5 | 28 | 14 | 7 | 38 | 19 | 9 |

10420-4-4.23 HAYNES

*Here's a chart that gives you approximate charging times for particular charging rates, battery ratings and battery states of charge*

don't fast charge unless you're in an emergency situation and must have the battery charged right away. If you choose to fast charge, monitor the battery carefully to avoid overcharging *(see illustration)*. Don't let the temperature get over 50°C (125° F) and watch for spewing of electrolyte.

A cold battery (below 4° C or 40° F) won't readily accept a charge. When a fast charger is connected to a cold battery, the charging rate will be low at first, then increase as the battery temperature increases.

## Troubleshooting the starting system

Most of the time, starting system problems aren't caused by the starter motor. They're caused by malfunctions elsewhere in the starting system, such as a discharged or defective battery, a bad battery cable connection or a weak or non-functional starter solenoid.

Listed below are the four most common starting system malfunctions, followed by procedures to help you identify the cause(s).

### The starter rotates, but the engine doesn't

Remove the starter, check the overrunning clutch and bench test the starter to make sure the drive mechanism extends fully for proper engagement with the flywheel ring gear (see Overhauling starter motors below). If it doesn't, disassemble the starter to locate the problem.

Check the flywheel ring gear for bent areas, missing teeth and other damage. With the ignition turned off, rotate the flywheel so you can check the entire ring gear.

### The starter is noisy

If the solenoid is making a chattering/clicking noise, first check the battery (see Battery testing above). If the battery's OK, check the cables and connections and perform the voltage drop and current draw tests described in the

procedures below. If you have not located the problem, check the solenoid (see the procedure below).

If you hear a grinding, crashing metallic sound when you turn the key to Start, check for loose starter mounting bolts. If they're tight, remove the starter and inspect the teeth on the starter pinion gear and flywheel ring gear. Look for missing or damaged teeth.

If the starter sounds fine when you first turn the key to Start, but then stops rotating the engine and emits a zinging sound, the problem is probably a defective starter drive that's not staying engaged with the ring gear. Replace or overhaul the starter.

If the starter makes a high-pitched whine or clanging sound while it's rotating the engine, the clearance between the pinion gear and flywheel ring gear is probably incorrect. To check it:

a) *Disconnect the negative battery terminal, then remove the flywheel cover (where fitted) and pull the starter drive out to mesh it with the ring gear.*

b) *Check the clearance between the gears. Generally, the pinion teeth should engage the flywheel teeth about 3/4 of the way down from the top of each tooth. As an approximate indication, ther should be a clearance of about 0.5 mm (0.020-inch) between the teeth, which can be checked with a wire-type gauge. Check the clearance at several locations around the circumference of the flywheel. This will help you identify if the flywheel is bent or has runout.*

c) *On most other vehicles, the clearance is not adjustable. You must replace the component causing the problem (usually the starter drive).*

If the starter makes a high-pitched whine after the engine starts, as the key is being released, the return spring in the starter is weak or the pinion gear-to-ring gear clearance is too small. Check the clearance as described above. If it's OK, replace the return spring. On some starters, the spring is located inside the solenoid. On others, it's located within the starter.

## The starter rotates slowly

Check the battery (see Battery testing above).

If the battery is okay, verify all connections (at the battery, the starter solenoid and motor) are clean, corrosion-free and tight. Make sure the cables aren't frayed or damaged.

Check to see if the battery cables are the same gauge (thickness) as original equipment. Many inexpensive aftermarket cables use a smaller gauge wire encased in thick insulation. They look as big in diameter as the original equipment cable, but their smaller diameter wire can't handle the amperage load. During the summer, when cranking loads are lighter, these cables may work OK. But when winter arrives, they often can't carry enough current and the starter rotates slowly. If you doubt any of the cables, check for a voltage drop (see the procedure below).

Check the voltage drops at the battery terminals, starter solenoid and starter connections (see the procedure below).

Check that the starter is bolted securely to the engine so it earths/grounds properly. Also check the pinion gear and flywheel ring gear for evidence of a mechanical bind (galling, deformed gear teeth or other damage).

Check for a short to earth/ground.

Perform a current draw test.

If the current draw is excessive, and there are no excessive voltage drops in the starter circuit, either the starter is defective or there is a mechanical bind in the engine. With the ignition turned to OFF, rotate the engine through two revolutions by hand. If it rotates smoothly and easily, replace the starter.

## The starter does not rotate at all

Turn on the headlights and turn the key to Start. Have an assistant observe the headlights. If the headlights do not dim when you turn the key, check for an open in the starting system, as described in the procedure following this one. If the headlights dim, continue with this procedure.

Check the battery (see *Battery testing* above).

If the battery is okay, verify all connections (at the battery, the starter solenoid and motor) are clean, corrosion-free and tight. Make sure the cables aren't frayed or damaged.

Check the starter solenoid (see the procedure below).

Check to see if the battery cables are the same gauge as original equipment. If you doubt any of the cables, check for a voltage drop as described in the procedure below.

Check for a voltage drop at the battery terminals, starter solenoid and starter connections (see the procedure below).

Check that the starter is bolted securely to the engine so it earths/grounds properly. Also check the pinion gear and flywheel ring gear for evidence of a mechanical bind (galling, deformed gear teeth or other damage).

Check for a short to earth/ground.

Test the starter current draw, as described below. If the current draw is excessive, and there are no excessive voltage drops in the starter circuit, the starter is defective or there is a mechanical bind in the engine. With the ignition turned to OFF, rotate the engine through two revolutions by hand. If it rotates smoothly and easily, replace the starter.

## Testing for an open in the starter circuit

⊘ *Warning: The starter may operate during the following tests, so make sure the vehicle is not in gear and stay away from components that move during engine operation.*

**Note:** *The battery must be in good condition and fully charged for the following tests (see Battery testing above).*

Check the starter solenoid (see below).

If the solenoid check reveals no voltage at the control circuit wire, check the neutral start switch or the clutch interlock switch – if equipped (see below). If the switch tests good, the open is in the ignition switch or in the wiring between the fuse panel and the control circuit terminal on the solenoid.

If the solenoid check reveals the solenoid is operating normally, have an assistant hold the ignition key in the Start position. Check for voltage along the cable running to the starter, beginning at the battery. When you reach a point where you find no voltage, the open lies between that point and your last test point.

## Checking for voltage drops

⊘ *Warning: The starter may operate during the following test, so make sure the vehicle is not in gear and stay away from components that move during engine operation.*

**Note:** *Chapter 3 contains additional information on checking for voltage drops.*

In the starting system, the most common places for voltage drops to occur are at the cable connections at the battery, solenoid and starter, and along the cables *(see illustration)*.

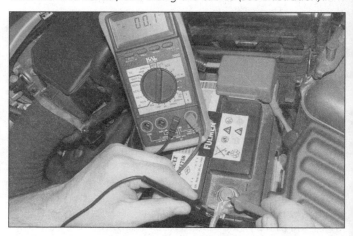

*Here a battery cable connection at the battery is being checked for a voltage drop*

**Here are the terminals on a typical on-starter solenoid**
1 Battery cable terminal   2 Control circuit terminal   3 Starter motor strap

**Here's typical clutch interlock switch – mounted under the dash, at the top of the clutch pedal arm**

Have an assistant turn the key to Start while you check for a drop at each of these locations. There should be no more than a 0.1 volt drop at any connection or along any one-foot length of cable. There should be no more than a 0.5 volt drop between the battery and the starter.

## Testing the starter solenoid

**⚠ Warning:** *The starter may operate during the following tests, so make sure the vehicle is not in gear and stay away from components that move during engine operation.*

**Note:** *The battery must be fully charged and in good condition for the following tests (see Battery testing above).*

Have an assistant turn the ignition key to Start while you listen for a click at the solenoid.

If there's no click, remove the control circuit wire (the small wire) from the solenoid terminal. Check for corrosion, looseness or other causes of a bad connection.

**Note:** *Some solenoids have two small-wire connections. One is for the solenoid's control circuit; the other bypasses an ignition resistor during starting. The one for the solenoid control circuit is often marked 'S.' If you're not sure which connection is which, check the wiring diagram for the vehicle.*

If the click is weak or the solenoid chatters, connect a jumper wire between the battery positive terminal and the solenoid's control circuit connection. A solid click indicates normal solenoid operation. If there's no click, or if the click is weak or the solenoid chatters, check for a loose solenoid, corrosion at the solenoid base or other causes of a bad solenoid earth/ground. If the solenoid is tight and earthed/grounded properly, and it still doesn't click, replace the solenoid.

While an assistant turns the key to Start, check for voltage at the control circuit wire with a voltmeter *(see illustration)*. If

there's no voltage at the wire, there's an open circuit in the in the circuit to the solenoid (see *Testing for an open in the starting circuit* above). Re-connect the control circuit wire.

Have an assistant turn the key to Start while you check for a voltage drop between the battery cable terminal and the starter motor strap. The voltage drop should not exceed 0.2 volts. If it does, replace the solenoid.

## Testing the starter inhibitor/neutral start switch

A quick check for the neutral start switch is to place your foot firmly on the brake and hold the ignition key to Start while you move the selector lever through all its positions. If the starter operates in positions other than Park and Neutral, the neutral start switch is damaged or out of adjustment.

To more completely check the switch, remove its electrical connector and connect a jumper wire between the terminal of the connector that receives battery voltage and the terminal that leads to the starter solenoid. If the starter now operates normally, adjust or replace the switch.

**Note:** *Starter inhibitor/Neutral start switch designs vary, and many incorporate reversing light switches. To properly check the switch, you may need to obtain the wiring diagrams for the vehicle. Also, check any specific procedures in the Haynes Service and Repair Manual written for your vehicle.*

## Testing the clutch interlock switch

When fitted, the clutch interlock switch is normally located under the dash, near the top of the clutch pedal arm *(see illustration)*. If the switch has two wires connected to it, remove its electrical connector and attach a jumper wire between the two terminals of the connector. If the switch has one wire, remove the connector and attach a jumper wire between the connector terminal and earth/ground. If the starter now works normally, adjust or replace the switch.

## Testing starter current draw

This test will tell you how much current is being drawn by the starter motor, cables and solenoid. It requires use of an inductive pick-up ammeter *(see illustration)*. This tool is available inexpensively from car accessory/tool shops.

> (!) *Caution: Never operate the starter motor for more than 10 seconds at a time without pausing to allow it to cool down for at least two minutes. Overheating caused by excessive operation will seriously damage the starter motor.*

Check that the battery is fully charged and in good condition (see *Battery testing* above). If it's not, this test will not be accurate.

The engine must be prevented from starting. Disable the fuel and/or ignition systems. On petrol vehicles, disconnect the low tension wire supplying electrical power to the ignition coil(s), and remove the fuel pump fuse. On diesel vehicles either disconnect the wire to the engine stop solenoid fitted to the injection pump, or disconnect the wiring plugs from the fuel injectors (engines with electronic diesel control). **Note:** *On petrol vehicles, do not operate the starter for more than a few seconds, as excess unburnt fuel will enter the exhaust system and may damage the catalytic converter.*

In accordance with the manufacturer's instructions, connect an inductive pick-up ammeter to the positive or negative battery cable.

Have an assistant in the vehicle operate the starter for a few seconds. Observe the ammeter scale. The reading shouldn't exceed 110 amps for a four-cylinder engine, 200 amps for a six-cylinder or small V-8 and 250 amps for a large V-8.

Re-enable the ignition/fuel systems.

## Starter motor removal and installation

**Note:** *Before removing the starter motor for repairs, be sure you have checked the other components in the starting system, as described earlier in this Chapter. Remember, most starting system problems are caused by the battery, cables and bad connections. The starter motor is seldom the culprit. This procedure is applicable to most vehicles. However, check the Haynes Service and Repair Manual for your vehicle. It contains specific procedures which might vary from these.*

Detach the cable from the negative battery terminal (see 'Battery disconnection' earlier in this Chapter).

Raise the vehicle and place it securely on axlestands.

Remove the engine undershield (where fitted).

Remove the front exhaust pipe if it prevents access to- or removal of the starter motor.

*Digital multimeters can be supplied with inductive clamps to measure amps*

Detach the wires from the solenoid. Note which wires are connected to which terminals. If this does not appear self-evident by wire colour and size, label the wires to prevent confusion during reassembly.

Remove the nuts and/or bolts which attach the starter to the engine and/or transmission bellhousing. If any of the nuts or bolts are shimmed, note the location and number of shims for each fastener.

Remove the starter from the engine. If there are shims beneath the starter, note how many so you can replace the same number on installation.

Installation is the reverse of removal.

## Starter motor overhaul

Once the starter is off the vehicle, clean it with degreaser and wipe it with a rag, then place it on a work bench.

Check the pinion for damage and rotate it. It should only rotate easily in one direction *(see illustration)*. If it rotates

*Check the starter pinion for freedom of operation by routing it in both direction with your fingers – it should only rotate freely in one direction*

*Check the armature for freedom of rotation by prying the pinion with a screwdriver – the armature should rotate freely*

*To do a no-lead bench test of the starter, connect a 12-volt battery – positive to the starter and negative to the starter case – connect a jumper wire or an old screwdriver (as shown here) between the battery terminal and the solenoid control circuit*

easily in both directions, and the armature does not move, the overrunning clutch is faulty.

Check the armature for freedom of rotation by rotating the pinion with a screwdriver in the overrunning clutch's locked position *(see illustration)*. Tight bearings or a bent armature shaft will prevent the armature from turning freely. If the armature can't turn freely, disassemble the motor immediately. If the armature does turn freely, perform a no-load test before you disassemble the motor.

The no-load test can point to specific defects which you can verify with further inspection when you disassemble the motor. You should also do a no-load test on a freshly overhauled motor prior to reinstallation, to verify that it operates properly.

To no-load test the starter, simply connect a 12-volt battery

as shown and bridge the solenoid terminals with a screwdriver *(see illustration)*. Don't run the starter for more than a few seconds at a time and make sure the battery is in good condition.

> ⚠ *Warning: Keep your fingers away from the rotating pinion gear!*

Follow the disassembly procedure photos for the type of starter you have. Inspection and testing procedures for the starter motor components follow the disassembly procedures.

## Typical Pre-engaged starter motor disassembly

**1**

*Disconnect the field strap from the terminal on the solenoid*

**2**

*Remove the bolts which attach the solenoid to the starter drive housing*

**3**

*Twist the solenoid clockwise . . .*

... and separate it from the starter drive housing – remove the return spring and set it aside

Remove the two solenoid cover screws

Remove the nuts from the motor terminal (usually marker 'B') and the switch terminal – terminal studs have welded leads, so avoid twisting the terminal when loosening the nut

Remove the solenoid cover and inspect the contacts – if they're dirty, clean them with the contact cleaner; if they're burned or damaged, replace the solenoid

Remove the two through bolts from the starter and remove the drive housing

Pull the armature and overrunning clutch assembly out of the field frame

Remove the commutator frame

*This is what the brushes, brush holders and springs look like when assembled properly*

*To remove the brushes, remove the small screw attaching the lead to each brush*

*Inspect the brushes for wear – replace the set if any are worn to one-half their original length. Judging from this brush, the brushes in this starter should be replaced*

*To remove the overrunning clutch from the armature shaft, remove the thrust collar from the shaft, slide an old socket onto the shaft so that it butts against the edge of the retainer, then tap the socket with a hammer and drive the retainer towards the armature and off the circlip*

*Remove the circlip from its groove in the shaft with a pair of pliers or a screwdriver – if the circlip is badly distorted , use a new on during reassembly*

*Slide the retainer off the armature shaft*

*Slide the drive assembly off the shaft – reassembly of the starter is the reverse if disassembly*

# Chapter 4

1

Unscrew the two through bolts

2

Remove the end plate

3

Separate the two halves of the starter and remove the brush terminal screw

4

Pull out the armature assembly

5

Remove the brush springs (arrowed)

6

Pull the brushes out with a pair of needle nose pliers

Remove the washer

Remove the thrust washer

Remove the brush holder screw (arrowed)

Remove the brush holder and solenoid assembly

Remove the spring from the plunger

Remove the nut

Remove the insulator washer

De-solder the shunt coil lead

Separate the solenoid from the brush holder assembly

Remove the plunger assembly

Remove the clip (arrowed) from the plunger

Remove the small washer from the plunger

Remove the contact (big) washer from the plunger – inspect it for wear and, if worn, flip it over on reassembly; if it's worn on both sides, replace it

Remove the solenoid core from the housing

Pry the cover from the housing

Remove the retainer from the gear reduction shaft

Pull out the gear reduction shaft far enough to remove this washer-clip-washer trio (arrowed) – don't forget the order in which they are installed

Pull out the gear reduction shaft a little farther and remove the clutch and actuator assemblies (arrowed) – be sure to note how they're installed before removing them

Pull the gear reduction shaft out a little further and remove the gear

Remove the ring (arrowed) and remove the gear reduction shaft

Remove the cotter pin from the housing

Remove the actuator fork from the housing – be sure to note how it's installed before you remove it – reassembly of the starter is the reverse of disassembly

## Starter motor inspection and testing

### Inspection

**Note:** *Many automotive electrical specialists offer free starter motor testing and inspection. If the starter motor is in need of repair, it may be more economical to obtain a reconditioned/exchange unit rather than attempt to repair/overhaul the original.*

Clean the overrunning clutch with a clean cloth. Clean the armature and field coils with electrical contact cleaner and a brush. Do not clean the clutch, armature or field coils in a solvent tank or with degreasing solvents – they'll dissolve the lubricants in the clutch and damage the insulation in the armature and field coils. If the commutator is dirty, clean it with fine sandpaper. Never use emery cloth to clean a commutator.

Test the operation of the overrunning clutch. The pinion should turn freely in the overrunning direction only. Check the pinion teeth for chips, cracks and excessive wear. Replace the clutch assembly if damage or wear is evident. Badly chipped pinion teeth may indicate chipped teeth on the flywheel ring gear. If this is the case, be sure to check the ring gear and, if necessary, replace it.

Inspect the brushes for wear. Replace them as a set if any are worn to one-half their original length. The brush holders must hold the brushes against the commutator. Make sure they're not bent or deformed.

Check the fit of the armature shaft in the bushings at each end of the motor housing. The shaft should fit snugly in the bushings. If the bushings are worn, replace them or obtain a rebuilt starter motor.

### Testing the Armature

Check the commutator for wear. If it's heavily worn, out-of-round or the insulation strips between each segment are high, the armature should be turned on a lathe and the insulation strips should be undercut. This operation is best performed by a properly equipped automotive engineering workshop that's familiar with the procedure. It may be quicker and easier to obtain a rebuilt starter.

Using an ohmmeter or a continuity tester, check for short circuits between each commutator segment and the armature *(see illustration)*. Replace the armature if there are any shorts.

Using an ohmmeter or a continuity tester, check for continuity between each commutator segment and the segment to its immediate right and left. There should be continuity. If there's no continuity, there's an open circuit in the winding. The most likely places for an open circuit to occur is at the points where the armature conductors join the commutator segments. Inspect these points for loose connections. Poor connections cause arcing and burning of the commutator segments as the starter motor is used. If the segments aren't too badly burned, the damage can often be repaired by resoldering the conductors to the segments and

*Checking for a short between a commutator segment and the armature – note how each commutator segment and associated armature winding are joined by a conductor (arrowed)*

cleaning up the burned material on the commutator with sandpaper.

Short circuits are sometimes produced by carbon or copper dust (from the brushes) between the segments. They can usually be eliminated by cleaning out the slots between the segments. If a short cicrcuit persists, you'll need to take the armature to a properly equipped workshop to be tested on a growler. Often, it's easier to simply obtain a rebuilt starter.

Check for earths/grounds. These often occur as a result of insulation failure brought about by overheating the starter motor by operating it for extended periods. They can also be caused by an accumulation of brush dust between the commutator segments and the steel commutator ring. Earths/grounds in the armature and commutator can be detected with an ohmmeter or a continuity checker. Touch one probe of the test instrument to the armature shaft and touch the other probe to each of the commutator segments *(see illustration)*. If the instrument indicates continuity at any of the segments, the armature is earthed/grounded. If

*Checking the armature and commutator for an earth*

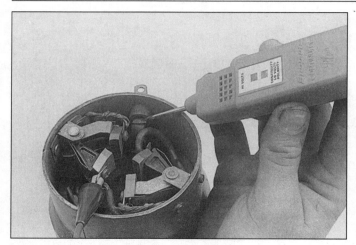

*Checking for an open circuit in the field coils*

*Checking for an earthed field coil*

cleaning won't correct the earth/ground problem, replace the armature (often it's easier to simply obtain a rebuilt starter).

## Field coils

**Note:** *Some European manufacturers now use permanent magnets instead of field coils.*

Using an ohmmeter or a continuity tester, place one probe on each field coil connector *(see illustration)*. The instrument should indicate continuity. If there's not continuity, there's an open circuit in one of the field coils. It's best to obtain a rebuilt starter, since field coil replacement normally requires special tools.

Place one probe of an ohmmeter or continuity tester on one of the field coil connectors. Place the other probe on the starter frame *(see illustration)*. Disconnect the shunt coil earth/ground, if applicable, before you do this check. If the instrument indicates continuity, the field coils are earthed/grounded; obtain a rebuilt starter.

# Charging systems

## General information

The charging system includes an alternator, a voltage regulator, a charge indicator light or gauge (see Chapter 7), the battery (see Chapter 4), a fusible link (see Chapter 1) and the wiring between all the components. The alternator is normally driven by a drivebelt at the front of the engine.

This Chapter focuses on alternator-type charging systems since they are used on all modern vehicles.

The alternator produces current used to charge the battery and operate the vehicle's electrical system during engine operation.

The voltage regulator limits the alternator voltage to a preset value. This prevents power surges, circuit overloads, etc., during peak voltage output from the alternator. The voltage regulator is usually integral with the alternator.

If the vehicle is equipped with a charge indicator light, it should come on when the ignition key is turned to ON, then immediately go out after the engine is started. If the vehicle is equipped with a voltmeter, it should normally indicate between 13 and 15 volts (12-volt system) when the engine is operating. If the vehicle is equipped with an ammeter, it should normally remain at or near the neutral position (not showing a significant charge or discharge) when the engine is operating. If the indicator light or gauge is not operating as described, there may be a problem in the charging system.

Be very careful when making electrical circuit connections to a vehicle equipped with an alternator and note the following:

a) *When reconnecting wires to the alternator from the battery, be sure to note the polarity.*

b) *Before using arc welding equipment to repair any part of the vehicle, disconnect the wires from the alternator and the battery terminals.*

c) *Never start the engine with a battery charger connected.*

d) *The alternator is driven by an engine drivebelt which could cause serious injury if your hand or clothes become entangled in it with the engine running.*

e) *Because the alternator is connected directly to the battery, it could arc or cause a fire if overloaded or shorted out.*

f) *Wrap a plastic bag over the alternator and secure it with rubber bands before steam cleaning the engine.*

*A typical alternator, disassembled*

| 1 | End frame | 4 | End frame | 8 | Brush holder |
|---|-----------|---|-----------|---|--------------|
| 2 | Stator and diode | 5 | Fan pulley | 9 | Bearing retainer |
|   | plate | 6 | Bearing | 10 | Bearing |
| 3 | Rotor | 7 | Brushes | | |

## Alternators – basic theory of operation

The alternator is a device that converts mechanical energy into electrical energy, providing current to charge the battery and power other electrical components on the vehicle.

Many older (mostly pre-1970s) vehicles use dynamos. Modern vehicles are equipped with alternators to handle the higher current demands of today's electrical systems. Alternators are lighter in weight, have a higher peak current capacity and produce more current at lower rotational speeds than dynamos.

Alternators produce current by creating motion between a conductor and a magnetic field. The principles of electromagnetism (discussed in Chapters 1 and 4) control how this current is produced.

In an alternator, the rotor (which creates the magnetic field) spins inside the stator (the conductor). Alternating current (AC) is induced in the stator, then changed to direct current (DC) by a diode bridge (rectifier) so it can be used in the vehicle's electrical system *(see illustration)*. The process of converting AC to DC is know as *rectification*.

## Maintenance

The alternator drivebelt, wiring, connections and mounting bolts should be checked every six months or 6000 miles, as discussed below. Battery maintenance should be performed every three months or 3000 miles (see Chapter 4).

### Drivebelt check, adjustment and replacement

Various types of drivebelts are used to drive the alternator. The drivebelt is normally located at the front of the engine. The condition and tension of the drivebelt are critical to the operation of the alternator. Excessive tension causes bearing wear, while insufficient tension produces slippage, noise, alternator vibration and belt failure. A slipping belt is a common cause of a malfunctioning charging system (undercharging). Because of their composition and the high stresses to which they are subjected, drivebelts stretch and deteriorate as they get older *(see illustration)*. As a result, the

*Here are some of the common problems associated with drivebelts (check the belts very carefully to prevent untimely breakdown)*

**ACCEPTABLE**

Cracks Running Across
"V" Portions of Belt

1/2"

Missing Two or More Adjacent
Ribs 1/2" or longer

**UNACCEPTABLE**

Cracks Running Parallel
to "V" Portions of Belt

*Small cracks in the underside of a serpentine belt are acceptable – lengthwise cracks or missing pieces are cause for replacement*

alternator drivebelt (as well as other engine drivebelts) must be periodically checked and where necessary, adjusted.

Late models alternators are driven by a Poly-Vee or multi-ribbed . These are often referred to as serpentine belts because of the winding path they follow between various drive, accessory and idler pulleys.

### Check
With the engine off, open the bonnet and locate the alternator drivebelt at the front of the engine. Using your fingers (and a torch, if necessary), move along the belt, checking for cracks and separation of the belt plies. Also check for fraying and glazing, which gives the belt a shiny appearance. On Poly-Vee belts, also check for separation of the ribs from the rubber, torn or worn ribs and cracks in the ridges of the ribs *(see illustration)*. Both sides of the belt should be inspected, which means on ordinary V belts, you'll have to twist the belt to check the underside *(see illustration)*. Never twist a Poly-Vee (multi-ribbed) belt through an angle greater than 90° or the belt internal structure may be damaged. Use your fingers to feel a belt where you can not see it. If any of the above conditions are evident, replace the belt.

The most accurate way to check drivebelt tension is to use a special drivebelt tension gauge *(see illustration)*. Many manufacturers recommend using a special gauge to check tension on their vehicles (particularly vehicles using Poly-Vee (multil-ribbed) belts). For specifications and special procedures, check the Haynes Service and Repair Manual written for your particular vehicle.

**Note:** *Some vehicles are equipped with an automatic*

*On ordinary V-belts, be sure to twist the belt to inspect the underside for cracks, fraying, etc*

*Where a specific belt tension is recommended by the vehicle manufacturer, several different devices are available from tools suppliers etc. They are often capable of displaying the tension in several different units of measurement. This one is an electronic tension gauge – the measuring head is arrowed*

J44875

*On some models the drivebelt is automatically tensioned and requires no service as long as it is in good condition and the indicator is in the proper range. When the groove (A) aligns with the mark (B) on the mounting bracket, the belt requires removal*

*tensioner which can be checked visually to make sure the indicator is in the proper range. Replace the belt with a new one when the indicator is out of the range specified by the manufacturer (see illustration).*

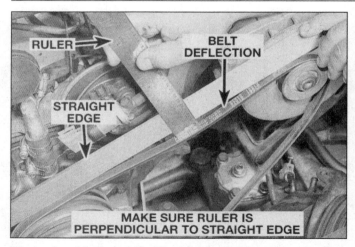

Measuring drivebelt deflection with a straightedge and ruler

On many vehicles, the alternator is held in place with pivot and locking bolts (arrowed)

If you do not have a special gauge, and cannot borrow one, the following method is recommended as an alternative. Lay a straightedge across the longest free span (the distance between two pulleys) of the belt. Push down firmly on the belt at a point half-way between the pulleys and see how much the belt moves (deflects). Measure the deflection with a ruler. The belt should deflect 6 mm (1/4-inch) if the distance from pulley center-to-pulley center is between 175 and 280 mm (7 and 11 inches); it should deflect 12 mm (1/2-inch) if the distance from the pulley center-to-pulley center is 300 to 400 mm (12 to 16 inches) (see illustration).

If the drivebelt tension or deflection is not correct, adjust it, as described below. If it's correct, check the alternator mounting bolts to be sure they're tight.

### Adjustment

**Note:** The following procedure is general in nature. For more specific procedures, check the Haynes Service and Repair Manual written for your particular vehicle. On some vehicles, the drivebelt is automatically tensioned and requires no service as long as it is in good condition and the indicator is in the proper range.

On many vehicles, the alternator is mounted by a locking bolt and a pivot bolt or nut (see illustration). Both must be loosened slightly to enable you to move the alternator to adjust the belt. After the two bolts have been loosened, move the alternator away from the engine (to tighten the belt) or towards the engine (to loosen the belt). On some vehicles, you can loosen or tighten an adjustment bolt or nut to move the alternator (see illustration). If there's no adjustment bolt or nut, move the alternator by hand; it may be necessary to use a special tool or some sort of a prybar. If this must be done, be very careful not to damage the alternator housing. When the tension is correct, retighten all bolts and nuts, starting with the locking bolt.

On some vehicles (particularly vehicles with serpentine belts), the belt is adjusted by moving a separate idler pulley (see illustration).

On some vehicles, after loosening the pivot bolt (A) and locking bolt (B), an adjustment bolt (C) can be used to adjust the drivebelt tension

Alternator drivebelt tensioner adjustment bolt (arrowed)

## Replacement

To replace the drivebelt, follow the procedures for drivebelt adjustment, but slip the belt off the pulleys and remove it. On vehicles with automatic tensioners, it's necessary to use a tool to rotate the tensioner against the spring pressure in order to releive the tension in the spring. Once in this position, on many automatic tensioners there is a facility to lock it in this position *(see illustration)*. Since belts tend to wear out more or less at the same time, it's a good idea to replace the other drivebelts at the same time. Mark each belt and the corresponding pulley grooves so the replacement belts can be installed properly.

Take the old belts with you when purchasing new ones in order to make a direct comparison for length, width and design.

Adjust the belts as described above.

When replacing a serpentine belt, make sure the new belt is routed correctly or the water pump could turn backwards, causing overheating. An illustration showing the drivebelt type and routing may be located in the relevant Service and Repair manual. Also, serpentine belts must completely engage the grooves in the pulleys.

## Wiring check

Next inspect the alternator wiring for cracking, deterioration, chafing or any other signs of wear *(see illustration)*. Replace any wires as necessary (see Chapter 3).

Disconnect the negative battery cable and check the tightness of all electrical connections on the alternator. **Note:** *Refer to 'Battery disconnection' in Chapter 4.*

*On many automatic tensioners, once the pulley has been moved away from the belt, the tensioner arm can be locked in place by inserting a pin through the appropriate holes*

*Inspect the wiring going to the alternator – if the vehicle has a split conduit like this, open it to expose the wires inside*

## Troubleshooting

If a malfunction occurs in the charging system, do not automatically assume the alternator is causing the problem. First check the following items:

a) *Check the drivebelt tension and condition, as described in the previous Section. Replace it if it's worn or deteriorated. If the drivebelt tension is correct, try turning the alternator pulley with your hand to see if the belt is slipping. If it slips, replace the belt (see illustration).*

b) *Make sure the alternator mounting bolts are tight (see the previous Section).*

c) *Inspect the alternator wiring harness and the connectors. They must be in good condition, tight and have no corrosion.*

d) *Check the fusible link (if equipped) or main fuse located*

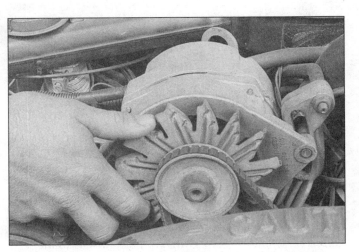

*With your hand, try turning the pulley to see if the belt slips*

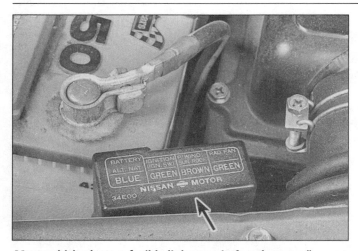

*Most vehicles have a fusible link or main fuse (arrowed)*

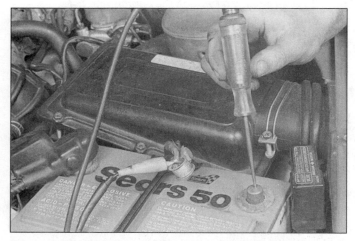

*Connect a test light between the negative battery post and negative battery cable*

*Connect a voltmeter to the battery – the black lead to the negative post and the red lead to the positive post*

*between the starter solenoid and alternator (see illustration). If it is burned, determine the cause, repair the circuit and replace the link or fuse (The vehicle will not start and/or the accessories will not work if the fusible link or main fuse is blown). Sometimes a fusible link or main fuse may look good, but still be bad. If in doubt, remove it and check for continuity.*

*e) Start the engine and check the alternator for abnormal noises (a shrieking or squealing sound indicates a bad bearing or belt slippage).*

*f) Check the battery (see Chapter 4). Make sure it's fully charged and in good condition (one bad cell in a battery can cause overcharging by the alternator).*

*g) Disconnect the battery cables (negative first, then positive). Inspect the battery posts and the cable clamps for corrosion. Clean them thoroughly if necessary (See Chapter 4). Reconnect the cables (positive first, then negative).*

*h) With the key off, connect a test light between the negative battery post and the disconnected negative cable clamp (see illustration).*

*1) If the test light comes on, there is a short (drain) in the electrical system of the vehicle. The short must be repaired before the charging system can be checked.*

*2) Disconnect the alternator wiring harness.*

*(i) If the light goes out, there's a problem in the alternator. Replace it.*

*(ii) If the light stays on, pull each fuse until the light goes out (this will tell you which component is shorted).*

*3) If the test light does not come on, reattach the clamp and continue the tests.*

Using a voltmeter, check the battery voltage with the engine off *(see illustration)*. It should be approximately 12.5 volts (12-volt system).

Start the engine, increase engine speed to approximately 2000 RPM and check the battery voltage again. It should now be approximately 14 – 15 volts.

Turn on the headlights. The voltage should drop, and then come back up, if the charging system is working properly.

If the voltage reading is more than approximately 15 volts, replace the regulator. Note that most automotive electrical engineers will carry out alternator checks and inspections free of charge. If the regulator is defective, it may be possible to replace just the regulator/rectifier assembly – refer to 'Alternator overhaul' later in this Chapter.

If the voltage is less than 13 volts, an undercharging condition is present. If the vehicle is equipped with a charge indicator light, turn the ignition key to ON and see if the light illuminates. If it doesn't, check the indicator light circuit (see Chapter 7). In some vehicles, a faulty circuit could cause the alternator to malfunction.

## Alternator – removal and installation

Disconnect the negative battery cable. **Note:** *Refer to 'Battery disconnection' in Chapter 4.*

Remove the drivebelt (see *Maintenance* above).

Detach all electrical connectors, taking note how they come off *(see illustration)*.

Remove the alternator mounting bolts and lift it from the engine compartment (see *Maintenance* above).

If you are replacing the alternator, take the old alternator with you when purchasing a replacement unit. Make sure the new/rebuilt unit is identical to the old alternator. Look at the terminals – they should be the same in number, size and locations as the terminals on the old alternator. Finally, look at the identification markings – they will be stamped in the housing or printed on a tag or plaque affixed to the housing *(see illustrations)*. Make sure these numbers are the same on both alternators.

Many new/rebuilt alternators do not have a pulley installed, so you may have to switch the pulley from the old unit to the new/rebuilt one. When buying an alternator, find out the shop's policy regarding installation of pulleys – some shops will perform this service free of charge. For further information on pulley removal see *Alternator Overhaul* (below).

Installation is the reverse of removal.

After the alternator is installed, adjust the drivebelt tension (See *Maintenance* above).

Check the charging voltage to verify proper operation of the alternator (See *Troubleshooting* above).

*Typical electrical connectors on an alternator*

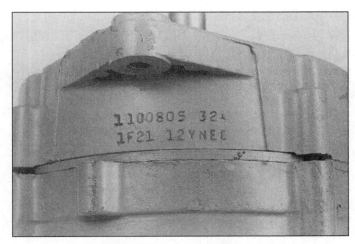

*On some types of alternators the identification numbers are stamped on the housing*

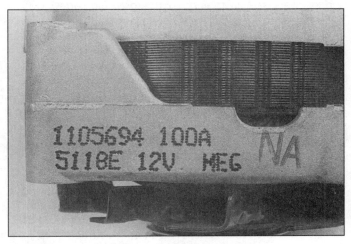

*Another type of stamped identification number*

*Some late model alternators cannot be rebuilt – they can be identified by special bolts (arrowed) or rivets*

*Paint or scribe a line across the length of the alternator housing to ensure correct reassembly*

## Alternator overhaul

**Note:** *Special tools are needed to overhaul an alternator. These tools include an ohmmeter, soldering gun and special pullers and installers. Before disassembling the alternator, check the availability and prices overhaul kits and also the prices of new and rebuilt alternators. Often, you'll find it easier – and sometimes less expensive – to obtain a rebuilt unit.*

### Disassembly

**Note:** *Some late model alternators are not intended to be disassembled and rebuilt. These usually have through-bolts with special heads or rivets in place of the through-bolts (see illustration).*

Scribe or paint a line across the alternator housing to ensure correct reassembly *(see illustration)*.

Remove the pulley. Some alternators require special pullers and installers *(see illustrations on the following pages)*. Do not try to pry off the pulley or you could damage the pulley or alternator housing. On other types of alternators, the pulley can be removed with common hand tools. After the pulley has been removed, some alternators will have a spacer. On some models, the brush holder and/or regulator should also be removed at this time.

Remove the housing through bolts.

Carefully separate the end frames. On some late-model alternators it is necessary to heat the rear end frame. This expands the end frame so it will separate from the rotor bearing.

On some models, the stator can be removed by removing three nuts on the inside of the rear housing. On other models, the stator and the diode plate must be removed as an assembly. On other models, the stator must be de-soldered for removal. If you remove the diode plate, take note of any spacers or insulators behind the plate.

Remove the brush holder and regulator.

Special pullers and installers are recommended to remove and install the bearings. However, the alternative methods described in the illustration captions work on some alternators.

**Note:** *Be extremely cautious when using the alternative methods – the bearings and aluminium end frames are easily damaged.*

### Inspection

After the alternator has been completely disassembled, clean all parts with electrical contact cleaner. Do not use de-greasing solvents; they can damage the electrical parts. Look for cracks in the case, burned spots and parts exhibiting signs of wear or other damage. Replace parts as necessary.

### Testing

With an ohmmeter, check the rotor for opens and grounds. Replace the rotor or obtain a rebuilt alternator if either condition is present.

If the rotor checks out OK, clean the slip rings with 400 grit or finer polishing cloth.

Check the stator for opens and grounds. Replace the stator or obtain a rebuilt alternator if either condition is present.

Check each diode or diode trio and rectifier bridge, as described in the accompanying illustrations. Replace any faulty parts.

### Assembly

Assembly is the reverse of disassembly.

Before installing the brush holder, insert a paper clip to hold the brushes in place during assembly. Remove the clip after assembling the alternator.

**1** On some alternators, special pullers are needed to pull off the fan pulley – sometimes, a standard puller can be substituted

**2** A press is needed to reinstall certain pulleys

On later vehicles fitted with high-output diesel engines, (normally common-rail), it's becoming common for the alternators to be fitted with an over-running drive pulley. This is due to the sharp crankshaft acceleration and deceleration pulses produced by these engines at low rpm. Theses pulses are transferred to the alternator causing high belt loads, belt slippage, high rates of belt wear and eventually belt failure. The overrunning pulley is a one-way clutch, which only transfers the acceleration pulses to the alternator, thus greatly reducing the forces transmitted by the belt, which dramatically increases belt life

H45348

**3**

**4** Damage to the fan pulley can occur if the wrong tool is used to remove or install the pulley

**5** Common hand tools can be used to remove some fan pulleys

After the fan pulley has been removed, some alternators will have a spacer

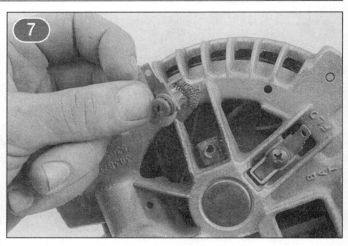

On some models the brushes can be removed without disassembling the alternator

To remove the regulator/brush holder assembly on this Motorcraft alternator, remove the four screws (arrowed)

On this Bosch alternator, the brush/regulator assembly is secured by two screws (arrowed)

On some, the plastic cover from the rear of the alternator must be removed (three screws – arrowed) . . .

. . . before unscrewing the brush pack

Remove the through bolts (arrowed)

Carefully separate the end frames

On some late model alternators, like this Mazda unit, it is necessary to heat the rear end frame with a 200 watt soldering iron to expand the rotor shaft bearing bore enough to separate the housings

On some models, you can remove three nuts (arrowed) and carefully separate the stator from the end frame

On some models, the stator and diode plate must be removed as a unit – remove the nuts (arrowed) . . .

. . . and carefully separate the stator and diode plate from the end frame

On some models, the stator must be de-soldered before removing it from the diode plate

After the stator/diode plate had been removed, take notes of any spacers or insulators as to where they go

If the stator and diode plate were removed as an assembly, carefully unsolder the connections

If the brush holder has not already been removed, remove it now – this holder is secured by two screws (arrowed)

This brush holder and regulator assembly is secured by two screws (arrowed)

Special tools are needed to remove some alternator bearings, but . . .

... sometimes a common two jaw puller can be used to remove the bearing – a hammer and socket the same diameter as the bearing inner race can be used to tap the new bearing into place

Here's still another method of removing and installing bearings. Place the end frame in a vice with one socket the same diameter as the bearing outer race and one larger than the outer race. When the vice is tightened, the bearing will be driven out. Use the same method to install the new bearing

A typical example of a burned out brush/regulator holder

A typical example of worn out brushes

A typical example of worn out slip rings

Check for continuity between the two slip rings – if there's no continuity, the rotor is open circuited and should be replaced

Check for continuity between each slip ring and the rotor shaft – if there's continuity, the rotor is earthed and should be replaced

Check for continuity between these two stator terminals . . .

. . . and these two – if there's no continuity, there is an open circuit in the windings and the stator should be replaced

Check for continuity between each stator terminal and earth – if there's continuity, the stator is earthed and should be replaced

If the alternator has diodes, connect an ohmmeter between each diode terminal and the diode case, then reverse the ohmmeter leads – if there's one high and one low reading, the diode is OK – if the readings are about the same, the diode should be replaced

If the alternator has a diode trio, connect an ohmmeter as shown, then reverse the ohmmeter leads – one high and one low reading indicates a good diode trio – if the readings are about the same, the diode trio should be replaced

If the alternator has a rectifier bridge like this, connect an ohmmeter as shown – one lead to the insulated heat sink (1) and the other to the metal clip; take a reading, then reverse the ohmmeter leads and take another reading – you should get one high and one low reading – if the readings are about the same, replace the rectifier bridge. Next, repeat this test with the other two clips, then repeat the entire test between the three clips and the earthed heat sink (2)

Before installing the brushes, insert a paper clip as shown, to hold the brushes in place during installation

After reassembly, simply pull the paper clip out

Where the alternator has a separate brush holder, compress the brushes then refit

# Notes

# Lighting systems

## General Information

The lighting circuits are among the most important parts of your vehicle's electrical system. They make night driving possible and alert others when you slow down or change direction. A properly operating lighting system is essential to being safe – and legal – on the road.

Fortunately, troubleshooting and repairing lighting system circuits is relatively easy. Most lighting failures are caused by blown fuses, burned out bulbs, corrosion and loose connections. On most vehicles, you can access lighting system components (with the exception of the turn signal switch) quickly and easily, using normal hand tools.

## Light bulbs

### General description

There are dozens of light bulbs in use on a typical vehicle today, illuminating everything from the road in front to the number plate in the rear (see illustration). Basically, a

*From the left, the first four bulbs have what's called a bayonet base – the positive contact(s) are on the bottom of the base and the earth/ground contact is the brass sleeve that forms the side of the base. Note that the second and fourth bulbs have two positive contacts – these are for the two filaments inside the bulb. The fifth bulb from the left is called a festoon bulb – its contracts are on either end of its glass tube. The bulb on the right is a press-in capless type. It has no base; its filament wires extend through the glass and serve as contacts*

*Here's an indication of a failed bulb – the dark-coloured residue inside the glass is from the filament evaporating*

*Here you can see the two filaments of a dual-filament bulb*

traditional bulb is nothing more than two posts (connected to the positive and negative contacts) with a thin strand of tungsten wire (called a filament) between them. When current flows through the filament, it heats up (due to resistance) and emits light. The glass dome over the bulb is used to contain the oxygen-free atmosphere necessary to keep the filament from burning out when it heats up.

Normally, it's easy to tell when a bulb has failed; either the filament will be broken or there will be a black or grey film on the inside of the glass dome (this is residue from evaporation of the filament) *(see illustration)*. However, the only way to be absolutely sure if a bulb's good is to remove the bulb and connect its positive and negative contacts to the battery using jumper wires (polarity is not critical – it can be connected either way). Use a fused jumper wire on the positive side to protect against a short circuit. If the bulb lights, it's good.

Some bulbs have two filaments, so the bulb acts electrically like two separate bulbs *(see illustration)*. These types of bulbs are commonly used for tail/braking light applications – one filament is the brake light and the other is the tail light. Both circuits of a dual-filament bulb must be checked before it can be considered good.

Some bulbs have no filaments. High-intensity gas discharge headlights are fitted to some late models. On these systems, the light is generated by an electric current (approx. 22 000 volts) arcing between two electrodes in a Xenon gas filled glass envelope – refer to the 'Headlights' Section for more information.

Further developments have seen LED (Light Emitting Diode) bulbs fitted as original equipment, and available as replacements for standard bulbs. There are several advantages to LED bulbs:

 a) *50 000 hour bulb life.*
 b) *Very low power consumption (1 watt typically).*
 c) *Greater resistance to vibration.*
 d) *Immediate on/off response.*

However, when replacing standard bulbs with LED items, because of the low power consumption, the vehicles electrical system may indicated a 'blown' bulb – either by a dashboard bulb monitoring system, or by increased indicator flash rate (or not flashing at all). To remedy this, it's necessary to place appropriate value resistors in series with the LED bulb, to mimic the electrical load of the standard bulb.

## Bulb replacement

### Brake, turn signal, tail light and reversing light bulbs

First, check to see if the bulb socket can be accessed from behind the lens. On rear-mounted bulbs, access is usually through the luggage compartment *(see illustration)*. You may have to remove a cover to get at the bulb socket. On front-mounted bulbs, you can usually access the socket by reaching down through the engine compartment. Often it's

*Once the cover in the luggage compartment is removed, the bulbholder are accessed on this VW Golf by squeezing together the retaining tabs (arrowed)*

*To access the headlamp bulb(s), it's often necessary to unscrew the access cover (Land Rover Freelander shown)*

*To remove a bulb socket, rotate it anti-clockwise 1/4-turn, then carefully pull it out*

necessary to remove a cover from the back of the headlight *(see illustration)*. On some the indicator is a separate assembly, and must be removed before gaining access to the bulb. Once you've reached the bulb socket, rotate it anti-clockwise about 1/4-turn and pull it out *(see illustration)*.

If there's no access to the bulb socket from behind the lens, there are normally screws along the outside of the lens. Remove the screws and pull the lens off *(see illustration)*. It may stick a little since there's a weather-sealing gasket behind it. If necessary, pry gently with a small screwdriver.

Once the bulb is exposed, push in and turn it about 1/4-turn anti-clockwise *(see illustration)*. If you're having difficulty turning the bulb, use a special bulb removal tool or protect your hand with a leather glove or a thick rag *(see illustration)*.

*Unscrew the retaining screws (arrowed) and remove the rear light cluster*

*To remove the bulb from the socket, push in firmly, then turn it 1/4-turn anti-clockwise*

*Bulb removal tools like this make removing bulbs safer and prevent breakage*

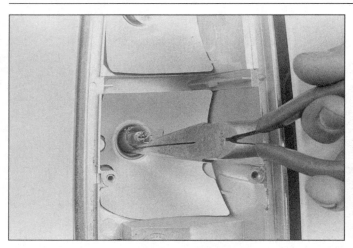

*If a bulb is broken, you can remove it with a pair of needle nose pliers*

*A special wire brush like this will remove corrosion from the bulb socket. Ensure all power to the circuit is turned off*

> ⚠ *Caution: Don't force a stubborn bulb by turning it with your bare hand. The stress of removal often causes bulbs to break, and your fingers could be severely cut when this happens.*

If the bulb is broken, remove the base of the bulb from the socket with a pair of needle-nose pliers *(see illustration)*.

Be sure to check the socket for corrosion, loose wires and worn or missing terminals. If the socket is corroded, clean it with a small wire brush *(see illustration)*.

Place the new bulb in the socket, aligning the indexing lugs with the slots in the socket. Press in firmly and rotate the bulb about 1/4-turn clockwise.

Double-filament bulbs normally have staggered indexing lugs, so, when installing the new bulb, be sure the indexing lugs match the socket *(see illustration)*. If the bulb does not rotate easily into place after pushing it firmly into the socket,

do not force it; you've probably got the indexing lugs in the wrong slots. Remove the bulb, rotate it 180-degrees and try again.

If the lens was removed, inspect the weather-sealing gasket to be sure it's not damaged. Replace it, if necessary.

**Side repeater lights**

Side repeater lights are normally removed by pressing the lens to the front, rear, or downwards *(see illustrations)*. This compresses the plastic clip, and allows the other edge of

*On dual-filament bulbs, the indexing lugs (arrowed) are staggered*

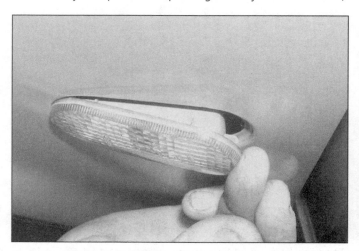

*Push the side repeater lens to the front or rear and prise out the other end*

*On some, the side repeater lens must be pushed downwards (Ford Focus shown)*

*Once the side repeater bulbholder is removed, the bulbs are normally capless and pull straight out of the holder*

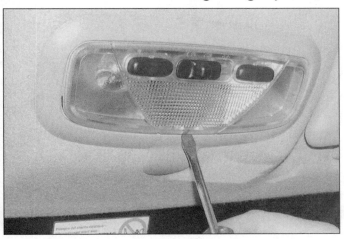

*Interior light lenses normally prise from place. Study them to identify exactly where the retaining clips are, to determine where to prise*

the lens to be prised out. Don't use too much force, the lenses are easily damaged.

Once the lens is removed, the bulbholders either rotate 1/4 turn anti-clockwise for removal, or pull straight out. The bulbs are normally capless, and are a push-fit in the holder *(see illustration)*. Be sure to check for corrosion, loose wires and worn or missing terminals.

Replacement procedures for number plate, courtesy, map, ash tray and other bulbs vary greatly from vehicle to vehicle. Inspect the lens and housing carefully to find the easiest method of removal. Bayonet type bulbs are removed by pushing in firmly and rotating the bulb 1/4-turn anti-clockwise. Festoon and capless type bulbs are removed by simply pulling them out *(see illustrations)*.

### High level brake lights

These lights are normally supplied with conventional bulbs, or LEDs (Light Emitting Diode). Whilst the LED equipped units will last much longer, when they do fail the complete assembly must be replaced.

In order to replace the traditional bulbs fitted to other vehicles, as the procedures vary so much from model to mode, it's essential that you refer to the appropriate Service and Repair manual for the instructions specific to your model. The bulbs fitted to the high-level lights tend to be of the capless type, and simply pull from the holders *(see illustration)*.

*Festoon bulbs are simply pulled from the contacts*

*The high-level brake lights may be fitted with capless bulbs that pull straight out of the bulbholder*

*Remove the cover (arrowed) from the rear of the headlight . . .*

*. . . disconnect the wiring plug . . .*

## Headlights

### General information

#### Sealed beams

Sealed beams are the traditional type of headlight, often fitted to British cars of the 60s and 70s, and some vehicles on the road today are still equipped with them. Depending on the design, a sealed beam uses either one or two tungsten filaments in a sealed glass case, which contains a non-oxygen atmosphere for the filament(s). Sealed beams containing one filament are used for the high beam. Sealed beams containing two filaments are used for both the high and low beams.

Depending on the number of filaments, a sealed beam has two or three spade terminals extending through its base. Dual-filament high/low beams have three terminals: one for high beam, one for low beam, and one for an earth/ground.

#### Headlights with separate bulbs

Since the mid 70s, most vehicles have been equipped with headlights that have separate, replaceable bulbs. These bulbs usually have tungsten filaments, surrounded by a halogen gas, enclosed in a glass or quartz envelope. Access to the bulbs is normally from the rear, without removing the headlight assembly – often a plastic cover must be removed to disconnect the bulb wiring plug(s). A retaining clip is then released and the bulb withdrawn *(see illustrations)*.

Some headlights are equipped with single filament bulbs or twin filament bulbs, where one filament is for the dipped beam, and the other for the main beam. When replacing defective bulbs, it's essential that they are replaced with same type. Whilst it may be possible to fit a replacement bulb of slightly higher wattage, or high output Xenon gas filled type, the new bulb must locate in the rear of the reflector in the same way as the old one *(see illustration)*.

*. . . and release the retaining clip*

*The locating lugs of the bulb must align with the corresponding slots in the reflector*

Two disadvantages of halogen bulbs should be noted:

1) *The bulb should not be handled because the salt from body perspiration will stain the quartz/glass: should the bulb be accidentally touched it may be wiped carefully, whilst cold, with methylated spirit and allowed to dry before use again*

2) *The life of the bulb is reduced rapidly if the quartz bulb and the gas filling are not maintained at the correct working temperature. A low supply voltage results not only in a drop in luminous power but also a serious fall in service life*

### Gas discharge headlamps

With gas discharge headlamps, light is generated by an electric arc between two electrodes in a small gas-filled glass tube. There is no filament *(see illustration)*. The light emitted from the lamp has high levels of green/blue components due to the composition of the gas (Xenon) in the tube.

Although there is a major increase in complexity and cost, the benefits of this system are:

a) *Increased service life (several times that of a normal halogen bulb)*

b) *Due to the design of the lens, reflector and aperture, a much longer and wider beam pattern is produced.*

c) *Output is upto 3 times that of a halogen bulb with no increase in power consumption.*

d) *No requirement for fog lights due to the wide near-field beam.*

A ballast/igniter unit supplies a high-voltage pulse of around 22 000 volts to initiate the electric arc between the

H45349

1 *Electrodes*
2 *Xenon filled glass tube*

*High-intensity Gas Discharge headlamp bulb*

bulb's electrodes. After the initial arc, an increased current is supplied for a few seconds until maximum brightness is achieved. Because of this delay gas discharge bulbs are normally only fitted to the dipped beams of the headlamps, a normal halogen bulb is used for the main beam.

To avoid dazzling oncoming motorists with the increased light output, vehicles equipped with gas discharge headlamps must also be fitted with an automatic headlamp levelling system. This systems alters the aim of the headlamps to compensate for any change in the vehicle load. The headlamp range ECU (Electronic Control Unit) monitors the vehicle loading via sensors fitted to the front and rear suspension, and alters the aim of the headlamps by means of electric motors connected via linkages to the headlamp reflectors *(see illustration)*.

*Headlamp self-levelling system*

1 *Headlight range control motor*
2 *ECU*
3 *Rear suspension height sensor*
4 *Front suspension height sensor*

H45350

*A typical headlight circuit*

When working with gas discharge headlamps, several safety aspects must be taken into consideration:

a) *Always disconnect the battery and allow any residual charge in the ballast/igniter to dissipate for a few minutes prior to commencing repairs.*

b) *The gas inside the bulbs is pressurised to in excess of 10 bar. Always were safety goggles when handling the bulbs.*

## Troubleshooting

When checking for a headlight failure, be sure to check the headlights on high and low beams. A two-filament light may have one of its filaments working, but the other may be burned out. Headlight circuits may have circuit breakers and/or fuses *(see illustration)*. Circuit breakers are normally located in the fuse panel or in the headlight switch. Some headlight systems have relays, either for the high beams only, or for both the high and low beams.

The most common failures are burned out or broken bulbs, blown fuses, corroded sockets and loose or dirty earth/ground wires. The following is a list of common failures and diagnosis strategies.

### One or more headlights don't work, but others do

☐ Check the fuse(s), look for corrosion at the fuse terminals and check for corrosion or a poor connection at the faulty light(s).

☐ If you haven't located the problem, connect a jumper wire between the earth/ground terminal of the non-functioning headlight and a good chassis earth/ground. Connect a fused jumper wire between the battery positive terminal and the positive terminal(s) of the headlight. If the headlight now works, check for a bad earth/ground. If the headlight does not work, replace it.

### No headlights work

☐ Check the fuse or circuit breaker and look for corrosion at the fuse or circuit breaker terminals. If the fuse continues to blow or the circuit breaker continues to cycle, check for a short circuit (see Chapter 3).

☐ If the vehicle has a headlight relay, check the relay. A quick (but not conclusive) check is to listen for a faint click when the headlight switch is turned on. To thoroughly check the relay, refer to Chapter 3.

☐ Check the dimmer switch.

☐ Check the headlight switch.

☐ Check for an open or short circuit (see Chapter 3).

### High or low beam works, but the other doesn't

☐ Check the fuse, look for corrosion at the fuse terminals and check for corrosion or a poor connection at the non-functioning light(s).

☐ If you haven't located the problem, connect a jumper wire between the earth/ground terminal of each non-functioning light and a good chassis earth/ground. Connect a fused jumper wire between the battery positive terminal and the positive terminals of each non-functioning light. If the lights now work, check for a bad earth/ground, then proceed to the next Step. If the lights still don't work, replace them.

☐ Check the high-beam relay (if equipped) (see Chapter 3).
☐ Check the dimmer switch.
☐ Check for an open or short circuit (see Chapter 3).

### Bulbs burn out quickly

☐ An overcharging (or undercharging – halogen bulbs) condition is indicated. Check the charging system (see Chapter 5).

### One headlight is dim, but others are normal

☐ Check for corrosion or a poor connection at the dim light.
☐ Check for a poor earth/ground connection.
☐ Check for excessive voltage drop in the wiring to the light (see Chapter 3).

### All lights go dim

☐ Check for a weak battery or a charging system malfunction (see Chapters 4 and 5).
☐ Check for corrosion at connections and other causes of high resistance in the headlight circuit.

### Lights flicker

☐ Check for loose or corroded connections at the headlights.
☐ Check for a loose or corroded earth/ground connection.
☐ If the vehicle has a circuit breaker, check for a short circuit (which would cause the circuit breaker to cycle).

### Lights glare, blinding approaching drivers

☐ Check for a problem causing the rear of the vehicle to ride lower than normal (i.e., low tyre pressure, incorrect tyres or wheels, sagging rear springs).

☐ Check the head light levelling switch is set correctly (refer to the Owners Handbook supplied with the vehicle).
☐ Adjust the headlights as described later in this Chapter.

## Headlight bulb replacement

### Sealed beam headlights

Remove the headlight bezel. In some cases, the bezel may be part of the vehicle's grille, so it may be necessary to remove the grille or part of the grille.

Remove the three or four screws that secure the headlight retainer (see illustration). DON'T disturb the (usually larger) headlight adjusting screws or the adjustment will be altered. Some vehicles have a spring attached to the retainer. Before removing the screws, use a hooked tool to detach it from the retainer. On some models with round headlights, you only need to loosen the retainer screws and rotate the retainer to disengage it from the screws.

Carefully remove the headlight retainer and pull the headlight out enough to unplug the connector behind it (see illustration). Remove the headlight.

Installation is the reverse of removal. Be sure the number on the lens is at the top. Check the headlights for proper operation and aiming before using them on the road. Normally, if the adjustment screws were not disturbed, the headlight will not need adjustment.

### Modern headlights

> ❗ Caution: The halogen bulb gets very hot in operation. Do not touch it while it's operating or shortly after it's been turned off. Don't remove the old bulb until a new bulb is ready to be installed. Leaving the bulb removed will allow dust and moisture to enter the headlight assembly and damage the reflector.

Open the bonnet and remove the access cover from the rear of the headlight (where fitted). Detach the electrical

*After removing the bezel, remove the headlight retainer screws – DON'T disturb the adjusting screws (arrowed) or the headlight aim will be altered*

*Once the retainer is removed unplug the headlight from its connector*

*Unscrew the headlamp rear cover . . .*

*. . . and disconnect the bulb wiring plug*

connector from the headlight bulbholder(s) *(see illustrations)*.

Release the bulb retaining clip *(see illustration)*.

Pull the bulb straight out of the socket *(see illustration)*. Do not touch the glass bulb. Hold it by the base.

Install the bulb so that its locating tabs align properly with the socket *(see illustration on page 6•6)*. Once the tabs are aligned, push the bulb into the socket. Refit the retaining clip, and reconnect the wiring plug(s)

Reinstall the rear access cover (where fitted) and check the lights for proper operation.

**Gas discharge headlights**

Replacement of a gas discharge bulb is essentially identical to the halogen bulb procedure previously described, with the following observations:

1) *Always disconnect the battery and then turn the lights on and off to allow any residual charge in the ballast/igniter to dissipate for a few minutes prior to commencing repairs.*

2) *The gas inside the bulbs is pressurised to in excess of 10 bar. Always were safety goggles when handling the bulbs.*

## Headlight aiming

Headlights must be aimed correctly. If adjusted incorrectly, they could dazzle the driver of an oncoming vehicle and cause a serious accident or seriously reduce your ability to see the road. The headlights are checked every 12 months as part of the MOT test in the UK, but should also be checked any time a new headlight is installed or front end body work is performed. The check and any subsequent adjustments only take a few moments, and will probably be carried out for a modest cost by the mechanic performing the check.

Although specialist equipment is required to accurately set the aim of the headlights, the following procedure is an interim step which will provide temporary adjustment until

*Release the retaining clip . . .*

*. . . then pull the bulb straight out*

the headlights can be adjusted using the proper equipment.

Before the headlights are adjusted, be sure there aren't any unusually heavy loads in the luggage compartment, the fuel tank is half-full and the tyres are inflated to the proper pressure.

Headlights have two adjustment screws: one controlling vertical movement and one controlling horizontal movement (see illustrations).

### Beam position aiming

Position the vehicle on a level surface, a 100 mm in front of a blank wall. The vehicle must be perpendicular to the wall.

Attach masking tape vertically to the wall in reference to the vehicle centreline and the centrelines of the headlights.

Now place a long piece of tape horizontally in reference to the centrelines of all the headlights.

Move the vehicle straight back to a point 7.5 meters from the wall.

Turn the headlights on and note the position of the high-intensity zone of the beams in relation to the tape marks.

On low beam, the high intensity zones should be 50 mm below the horizontal line and 50 mm to the left of the headlight vertical lines (see illustration). If you have a two-headlight system, you only need to adjust the headlights on low beam.

In a four-light system, the high and low beams are adjusted separately. Adjust the low beams as described above. To adjust the high beams, turn them on and note the position of the high intensity zones. They should be vertically centred, with the exact centre just below the horizontal line.

Adjustments are made by turning the adjustment screws as necessary to move the high intensity zones into their correct positions.

*Headlight horizontal adjustment screw (A) and vertical adjustment screw (B) – Ford Focus*

*Vertical adjustment screw (A) and horizontal adjustment screw (B) – VW Passat*

*Correct light pattern for RHD dipped headlight*

**Direction indicators and hazard warning lights**

H45351

## Typical turn signal and hazard warning lights circuit

1   Battery
4   Ignition switch
5   Fusebox
31  Combined horn and lighting switch
37  LH rear light unit
38  RH rear light unit
45  LH front direction indicator
46  RH front direction indicator
47  Direction indicator relay
48  Hazard warning switch
e   Direction indicator
b   Stop light
c   Reversing light
d   Direction indicator
b   Stop light
c   Reversing light
d   Direction indicator

# Turn signals and hazard warning lights

## General information

Hazard light circuits typically operate through the turn signal circuit. On older vehicles, a separate flasher unit, when activated by the hazard light switch, connects and disconnects all turn signal lights from the power source. On later vehicles, the functions of the turn signals and the hazard signals are incorporated into one flasher unit – often integral with the hazard switch.

There are several types of turn signal and hazard flasher units, but their basic function is the same (see illustrations). Their location varies from manufacturer to manufacturer, but they are often located on or near the fuse panel. On very recent vehicles, the timing function of the turn signal lights and the hazards is provided by one central timer unit (or generic electronic module – GEM) which also provides timing functions for the following:

a)  Courtesy lighting
b)  Heated windscreen
c)  Heated rear window
d)  Heated mirrors
e)  Windscreen wiping/washing
f)  Rear wiper/washing
g)  Seat belt warning
h)  Lights-on warning
i)  Door ajar warning
j)  Chimes warnings
k)  Central locking
l)  Tailgate/boot lid release
m) Alarm systems

**Old fashioned flasher unit**

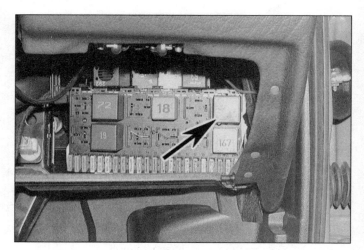

**Hazard/flasher relay (arrowed) – Seat Cordoba**

The central timer unit (or GEM) is equipped with a sophisticated self-diagnosis system, so if a fault is suspected, interrogate the system for any stored fault codes, using a fault code reader via the vehicle's diagnostic socket – refer to the appropriate Service and Repair manual or an automotive electrical specialist.

## Trouble shooting

The most common problems in the turn signal and hazard light circuits are burned out bulbs, blown fuses, defective flasher units and corroded or loose connections. The first step in diagnosing a failure is to visually check the lights. Operate the turn signal or hazard lights and walk around the vehicle, checking to see which lights are not working. Once you've identified the problem, check all the possible causes in the following list. If the symptom persists after checking all the possible causes, check the turn signal switch and wiring, as discussed in the procedure following the symptom list.

**Note:** *On some vehicles, the turn signal switch and hazard light switch (usually integrated into one unit) are wired separately, but the wiring between the switches and lights is shared. This makes checking the wiring between the switch and the signal lights simple. For example, if the turn signals do not work on one or both sides, but do work when the hazard lights are turned on, you know the wiring between the turn signal/hazard switch and the lights is good. The problem probably lies at the turn signal fuse, flasher or switch.*

### One turn signal light on one side doesn't work
☐ Check the bulb.
☐ Check for a corroded, worn or damaged bulb socket.
☐ Check for a bad earth/ground. Use a jumper wire between the earth/ground side of the turn signal bulb and a good chassis earth/ground.
☐ Beginning at the non-functioning light and working backward through the circuit, check for a short or open circuit (see Chapter 3).

### Hazard lights or turn signals light but don't flash
☐ Check the bulbs are of the correct wattage.
☐ Have LED bulbs been fitted? Because of the LED bulb's power characteristics, a resistor made need to be fitted in series with the bulb – check with your supplier.

### Turn signals don't light in either direction
☐ Check for a blown fuse.
☐ Check the turn signal bulbs.
☐ Check for corroded, worn or damaged bulb sockets.
☐ Check for a bad earth/ground. Use a jumper wire between the earth/ground side of the turn signal bulbs and a good chassis earth/ground.
☐ Replace the turn signal flasher.
☐ Check the turn signal switch (see below).
☐ Check for a short or open circuit (see Chapter 3).

### Front and rear turn signal lights on one side don't work
☐ Check the bulbs.
☐ Check for corroded, worn or damaged bulb sockets.
☐ Check for bad earths/grounds. Use jumper wires between the earth/ground sides of the turn signal bulbs and a good chassis earth/ground.
☐ Check the turn signal switch (see below).

### Flasher rate too fast or too slow
☐ Make sure the correct flasher unit is installed.
☐ Make sure the correct bulbs are installed.
☐ If the rate is too fast, check for an overcharging condition (see Chapter 5). If the rate is too slow, check for a weak battery or an undercharging condition (see Chapters 4 and 5).

### Indicator light(s) on dash panel don't flash (glow steadily)
☐ Check the signal lights with the circuit turned on.
☐ If the signal lights are also glowing steadily, replace the flasher unit.
☐ If the signal lights are not on, check the signal light bulb.
☐ Check for a corroded, worn or damaged bulb socket.
☐ Check for a bad earth/ground. Use a jumper wire between the earth/ground side of the non-functioning signal light(s) and a good chassis earth/ground.
☐ Beginning at the non-functioning light(s) and working backward through the circuit, check for an open circuit.

### Indicator light(s) don't work, but signal lights do
☐ Check for a burned out indicator light bulb, corroded socket or bad earth/ground connection.

### Turn signals work but hazard lights don't
☐ Replace the hazard flasher unit.
☐ Check for a faulty hazard flasher switch (these are often integral with the turn signal switch).

## Turn signal switch check and replacement
**Note:** *The check and replacement of the turn signal switch varies from vehicle to vehicle. Be sure to check the appropriate Haynes Service and Repair Manual for your particular vehicle. Before following this procedure, be sure you have checked all other possible causes of the failure (see above).*

### Check
Locate the correct wiring diagram for the vehicle. Determine which wire carries current from the turn signal flasher unit to the turn signal switch and which wires carry current from the switch to the turn signal lights.

# Chapter 6

*To access the signal switch connector, you may have to remove a cover below the steering column*

*Probing the back side of the switch connector with the test light*

Find the turn signal switch connector, located near the bottom of the steering column. You may have to remove a cover from below the column *(see illustration)*.

Find the terminals on the connector associated with wires you identified above.

Turn on the left turn signal.

Connect a test light to the back side of the terminals you identified above *(see illustration)*. Don't unplug the connector.

The test light should flash when you probe the terminal that supplies current to the switch. If it doesn't, there's an open in the circuit between the battery and the switch.

The light should also flash when you probe the terminals that carry current to the left turn signal lights. The light should not light when you probe the terminals that supply current to the right turn signal lights.

Turn on the right turn signal and repeat the previous test.

If the switch fails any of the tests, replace it.

### Replacement

The replacement procedures for turn signal switches vary greatly from vehicle to vehicle. The following procedure applies to many vehicles; however, you should always check the Haynes Service and Repair manual for your specific vehicle.

> **Warning:** *To avoid system damage and possible personal injury, do not perform this procedure on models equipped with airbags without being familiar with the airbag disarming and removal procedure detailed in the manual. If in doubt, take the vehicle to a dealer service department.*

Remove the steering wheel cover to expose the steering nut. In some cases, a small cover in the center simply pulls off. In other cases, screws at the back of the steering wheel secure the cover. Disconnect any wires running from the cover. Disconnect any wires running from the cover to the steering wheel. On models equipped with a drivers air bag,

follow the instructions given in the appropriate Service and Repair manual and remove the air bag module from the steering wheel *(see illustration)*.

Mark the relationship of the steering wheel to the steering shaft to ensure proper alignment on installation *(see illustration)*.

*Disable the air bag, then release the clips and remove the cover from the centre of the steering wheel*

*Before removing the steering wheel, make alignment marks (arrowed)*

Remove the steering wheel securing nut/bolt, then pull the steering wheel from the shaft. If the wheel is difficult to remove, use a puller to detach it from the shaft.

Remove the steering column upper and lower shrouds. These are usually secure by one or two screws, and may be clipped together *(see illustration)*.

Disconnect the wiring plugs from the turn signal switch. On some vehicles, the winscreen wiper switch and headlight dip/main switch is incorporated into one unit with the turn signal switch. **Note:** *On models equipped with a driver's airbag, the clockspring contact unit must be removed from around the top of the steering column – this <u>must</u> be carried out in accordance with the vehicle specific instructions provided in the appropriate Service and Repair manual.*

Some turn signal switches are clipped into place, whilst others a retained by a clamp or fixing screw. Release the fixing and remove the switch *(see illustration)*.

Installation is the reverse of removal, but note the following:

a) *Make sure the wiring harness is correctly routed.*
b) *Set the switch in the neutral position before sliding it over the shaft.*
c) *When installing the steering wheel, be sure to align the marks you made when you removed it.*

*Steering column shroud bolts (arrowed)*

## Brake lights

### General information

The brake light circuit has a switch mounted on the brake pedal or pedal support *(see illustration)*. On some vehicles, the switch may be mounted in the master cylinder and is hydraulically operated. As the brakes are applied, the switch contacts close, and current is supplied to the rear brake light bulbs.

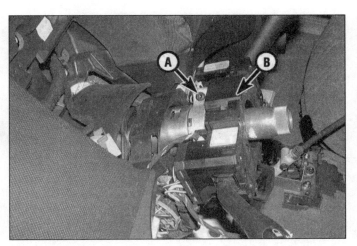

*Slacken the fixing screw (A) and slide the switch assembly (B) over the end of the column*

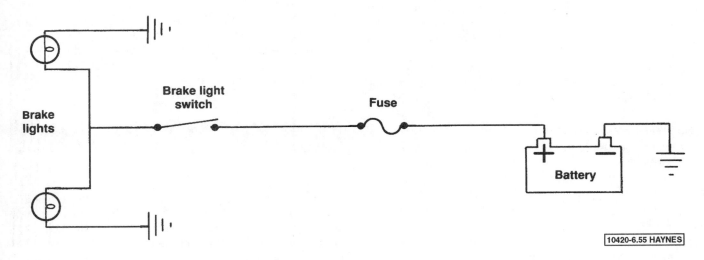

*A simple brake light circuit*

*Most brake light switches are mounted on the pedal arm assembly*

*Probing the terminal at the brake light switch with a test light*

Since the early 1990s many vehicles have been equipped with a third or high-level brake light mounted in the rear window or built into the rear of the vehicle.

Note that on some vehicles, the brake switch operation is also monitored by the engine management ECU (Electronic Control Unit). The ECU uses the information to determine when fuelling needs to be reduced during overrun conditions etc. Consequently, it is not unknown for an engine running fault to be caused by a defective brake light bulb!

## Troubleshooting

### One brake light does not work, but others do

☐ Check the bulb.
☐ Check the bulb socket for corrosion, damage and worn terminals.
☐ Check for a bad earth/ground connection by connecting a jumper wire between the negative terminal of the non-functioning light and a good chassis earth/ground. If the light now works, repair the faulty earth/ground connection.
☐ Beginning at the non-functioning light and working backward through the circuit, check for an open or short circuit (see Chapter 3).

### No brake lights work

☐ Check the fuse and check for corrosion at the fuse terminals.
☐ Check the brake light switch (see below).
☐ Check for a bad earth/ground at the brake light bulbs (see above), burned out bulbs and corroded or loose connections.

### Brake light bulbs burn out quickly

☐ Check for an overcharging condition (see Chapter 5).

## Brake light switch check

To find the brake light switch, check the Haynes Service and Repair Manual for your vehicle. On most vehicles, it's located on the brake pedal arm, on a bracket above the pedal arm or on the master cylinder *(see illustration)*.

If your vehicle has cruise control, there may be two switches or the brake light switch may have four terminals: two for the brake lights and two for the cruise control. If you're not sure which switch or terminals are for the brake light switch, check the wiring diagram for your vehicle.

After locating the brake light switch, probe the two terminals in the switch's electrical connector with a test light *(see illustration)*. The light should light when checking one of the terminals. It should not light when checking the other terminal. If it doesn't light at either terminal, there's an open or short circuit between the battery and the switch.

Use your hand to firmly depress the brake pedal and check the terminals again with the test light. This time, the light should light at both terminals. If it only lights at one terminal, the brake light switch must be adjusted or replaced. Check the Haynes Service and Repair Manual for procedures specific to your vehicle.

## Reversing lights

### General information

Reversing light circuits are almost identical to simple brake light circuits. They are operated by a mechanical switch that turns the lights on when the transmission is in Reverse. Switch locations vary from vehicle to vehicle, but most are mounted somewhere on the transmission casing (operated by a cam within the transmission) or the gearchange linkage

*This reversing light switch is mounted in the transmission case (arrowed)*

*This Ford starter inhibitor switch has an integral reversing light switch – it's mounted on the transmission case where the selector linkage connects*

*(see illustration)*. On some vehicles with an automatic transmission, the reversing light switch is mounted near or integral with, the starter inhibitor switch *(see illustration)*.

## Troubleshooting

Since reversing light circuits are highly similar to simple brake light circuits, the same troubleshooting procedures apply. The primary difference between the two types of circuits is that reversing light circuits are usually wired through the ignition switch, and the ignition switch must be on for the reversing lights to work. If the troubleshooting procedures listed in the Section on brake lights do not solve your problems, suspect a faulty ignition switch.

## Wiring a towbar

Wiring a towbar socket is straightforward providing you have the necessary tools available (wire strippers, crimpers etc.), and you allow plenty of time to fully understand what you're doing. If the towbar kit comes with its own instructions for wiring, follow them in preference to these. Although the following procedure description is for a Fiat Punto, it is general in nature and applies to the majority of vehicles. Note that the socket wiring details are standardised, and must be adhered to.

*Locate the electrical socket on the mounting plate and insert the retaining screws . . .*

*. . . then secure the screws with the retaining nuts*

Feed the socket wiring loom through the hole in the body rear panel into the luggage compartment

Insert the wiring loom through the rubber grommet

Cut the socket wiring cable sheath approximately 150 mm from the end . . .

. . . then remove the cut portion from the loom

Connect the two yellow wires together using an in-line connector . . .

. . . and crimp the connector securely using a crimping tool

Join the two earth wires together using a tag connector

Slide the earth wire tag connector over the junction box mounting stud . . .

. . . and secure with the retaining nut

Connect the towbar socket and audible warning unit wiring to the vehicle's harness using snap-crimp connectors

Attach the audible warning unit to a suitable place on the rear body panel

# Notes

# Indicator lights and gauges

## Introduction

The dashboard indicator lights and gauges are your 'eyes' into the vehicle's vital signs. They keep you informed of the operating conditions of the engine and electrical system. Instrument panels include various combinations of gauges and indicator lights. Most vehicles use an array of indicator lights in combination with a few gauges. Some instrument panels are equipped with gauges for every engine and electrical function, but they're usually found only on sportier or more expensive models. We'll look at gauges in a minute. First, let's look at some typical indicator light circuits.

### Indicator light circuits

An indicator light is usually nothing more than a small lens with a bulb behind it *(see illustration)*. Typically, it tells you

*A typical indicator light display uses a light behind a red lens with the type of problem or condition being indicated imprinted on the lens*

the nature of the warning with a printed statement (Door Ajar, Tail Lamp Out, etc.), or a small International Standards Organization (ISO) symbol (a petrol pump, a thermometer in water, etc.). This warning is printed on the dash immediately below each indicator light on older vehicles; on newer vehicles, it's usually printed right on the lens itself.

The sending unit in an indicator light circuit is a switch connected to a device that senses changes in oil pressure, coolant temperature or whatever parameter the sending unit is designed to monitor. The switch is normally open, but, when the parameter being monitored goes out of an acceptable range, the sensing device closes the switch contacts, completing the circuit to earth/ground and causing the indicator light to illuminate (see illustration).

Most indicator lights also illuminate when you turn the ignition key to On or Start. This 'self test' mode is designed to tell you the indicator light bulb and wiring are in good shape.

Indicator light circuits are normally very dependable, but when a problem does occur, the sending unit, wiring connections or light bulb is usually at fault.

## Oil pressure indicator light

Adequate oil pressure is critical to proper engine function, so most vehicles are equipped with some sort of oil pressure indicator light. The oil pressure indicator light on the dash is connected to an oil pressure sending unit on the engine (see illustrations). This sending unit contains a diaphragm which responds to changes in oil pressure. When oil pressure is below a pre-set value (usually about 0.3 bar), the switch is closed and the light on the dash is illuminated. When oil pressure rises above the pre-set value, the diaphragm opens

*A typical oil pressure sending unit for an indicator light – this Volkswagen unit is mounted at the rear of the cylinder head ...*

**A schematic of typical indicator light circuits**

1 Battery
2 Ignition switch
3 Fuse link wire
7 Diode
30 Instrument cluster
a RH indicator warning light
b LH indicator warning light
c Main beam warning light
d Temperature gauge with warning light
e Fuel gauge with warning light
f Voltage stabiliser
g No-charge warning light

h Oil pressure warning light
I Choke warning light
j ABS warning light
k Handbrake warning light
l Tachometer
m Instrument illumination
32 Coolant temperature sender
33 Fuel gauge sender
34 Oil pressure switch
35 Choke warning switch
36 Handbrake warning switch
37 Low brake fluid sender

*. . . this Peugeot unit is located above the oil filter on the front of the engine . . .*

*. . . and this Hyundai unit is located on the side of the engine block, below the exhaust manifold*

the switch, interrupting the indicator light's path to ground and turning off the light.

The oil pressure sending unit is located on the engine, usually high on the cylinder head or at the rear of the engine block, as far from the oil pump as the manufacturer could put it. Why so far from the pump? Because the farther it is from the pump, the lower the pressure. If pressure is good at the sending unit, it's usually OK anywhere in the lubrication system.

If the oil pressure light circuit is operating properly, the light should be illuminated when the ignition key is turned to On (engine off), then go out within a few seconds after the engine is started. If the light comes on during engine operation, turn off the engine immediately and locate the problem before returning the vehicle to normal service.

## Engine temperature indicator light

A safe operating temperature is also critical to proper engine operation. When engine coolant temperature rises too high (usually about 120° C), coolant boilover and major engine damage can occur. The engine temperature indicator light warns the driver when coolant temperature rises too high, allowing him to shut the vehicle down before major damage occurs *(see illustrations)*.

Most engine temperature indicator circuits function the same as oil pressure indicator circuits. The primary difference is in the sending unit, which is immersed in engine coolant. A bimetallic strip in the sending unit is sensitive to temperature changes and bends to close the sending unit contacts (and thus connect the indicator light to ground) when coolant temperature reaches a predetermined level.

*A typical coolant temperature sending unit for an indicator light – this Peugeot unit is located in the thermostat housing*

*This Ford unit is located in the end of the cylinder head*

Most modern temperature sender units are thermistors (a resistor that changes resistance as the temperature changes) instead of a potentiometer *(see illustration)*. The thermistor used has a low resistance at high temperature and a high resistance at low temperature.

## Low fuel level indicator light

Most vehicles are equipped with a fuel level gauge (which we'll get to in a moment). Some vehicles also have a special indicator light which turns on when the fuel tank is nearly empty, giving the driver an additional warning that the fuel supply is getting low.

The low fuel level indicator light circuit includes the warning light, a relay and a thermistor assembly in the tank. A thermistor is a special type of resistor that loses resistance as its heats up (just the reverse of a typical wire resistor). As long as there's enough fuel in the tank, the thermistor is submerged in the fuel and stays cool. But when the fuel drops below a certain level, the thermistor is exposed to vapours and starts to heat up. This allows more current to flow from the battery through the warning relay winding. The increased current flow through the relay winding produces a stronger magnetic field. When the field becomes strong enough to pull the relay contact points together, it completes the circuit from the battery to the indicator light, warning the driver that the fuel supply is low.

Low fuel level indicator circuits usually have a self-testing circuit to verify the light bulb, relay and wires are OK. When the ignition switch is turned to Start, a pair of contacts in the ignition switch connect the relay directly to the battery to turn on the warning light. If the light is malfunctioning, but comes on when the key is turned to Start, the problem is likely in the wiring to the thermistor or in the thermistor itself. If the light doesn't come on when the key is turned to Start, the bulb is burned out, the relay is defective or the circuit is open or shorted.

Some newer vehicles use an electronic low-fuel-level warning system. This system also has a fuel-level indicator light, but instead of using a thermistor in the tank, it monitors the voltage difference between the two terminals of the fuel gauge. As the needle moves toward E (empty), the voltage increases. When the tank is about one-eighth full, the voltage is great enough to turn on the low-fuel-level warning light *(see illustration)*.

## Charge indicator light

The charge indicator light is connected between the voltage regulator and the battery through the ignition switch. The indicator light is connected in parallel with a resistor. Current flows through the resistor and the indicator light on its way to the alternator field. The voltage drop through the resistor provides enough voltage to the indicator light to make the light glow. It glows until the engine starts and the alternator begins to charge the battery. When this happens, the voltage is the same on both sides of the resistor and the light. So the light goes off, indicating that

*A thermistor changes its electrical resistance as the temperature changes*

the alternator is charging the battery. On some vehicles, the light also comes on when charging voltage is too high. Note that – unlike temperature, pressure and low-fuel-level indicating circuits – the charge indicator light circuit has no sending unit.

## Bulb failure warning light

Bulb failure warning systems monitor the operation of low beam headlights, brake lights and tail lights. The arrangement of bulb failure indicators varies from one vehicle to another, but the basic operation of most systems is the same.

*Typical electronic low fuel level indicator circuit*

The major components in the system are the bulb failure warning module, special resistance wires and the indicator light(s). When all the lights being monitored are functioning properly, the special resistance wires provide about a 0.5 volt input to the bulb failure warning module. If one bulb goes out, the input of the resistance wire drops to about 0.25 volts. The bulb failure warning module detects this difference and completes a earth/ground path to the indicator light for the affected circuit. With battery voltage on the other side of the light, the light illuminates.

The bulb failure warning module is a solid-state unit designed to measure small changes in voltage levels. An electronic switch in the module closes to complete a ground path for the indicator lights in the event a light bulb burns out.

The resistance value of the special resistance wires is selected to compensate for the number of bulbs in the circuit. The length of these wires is extremely important to the overall operation of the system. Changing their length will hurt the system's performance.

## Troubleshooting indicator light circuits

The troubleshooting procedure for most indicator light circuits is pretty straightforward. Basically, indicator lights continuously receive voltage whenever the ignition switch is turned on. The circuit is completed to earth/ground whenever the sending unit contacts close, allowing current to flow through the light. **Note:** *Many late model vehicles have instrument clusters which have integral ECUs (Electronic control units) and LEDs instead of bulbs. The ECUs have sophisticated self-diagnosis capabilities, and should be interrogated for any stored fault codes with a fault code reader via the diagnostic plug. The LEDs are not available as separate items, and if faulty, the complete instrument cluster must often be replaced – check with your dealer.*

If no indicator lights work, check the fuse (see Chapter 1) and the wiring between the fuse panel and indicator lights. If you haven't identified the problem, suspect a faulty ignition switch.

### Oil pressure indicator light

#### The light on the dash comes on during engine operation
☐ Disconnect the wire at the sending unit.
☐ If the light is still on, there's a short to ground somewhere between the light and the sending unit.
☐ If the light goes off when the wire is disconnected from the sending unit, connect an oil pressure gauge into the fitting where the oil pressure sending unit is normally installed. Operate the engine and compare the pressure readings to the manufacturer's specifications.
    *a) If the oil pressure is within manufacturer's specifications, replace the sending unit.*

    *b) If the oil pressure is not within manufacturer's specifications, there's a mechanical problem causing low oil pressure.*

#### The light never comes on, even when the ignition is On (engine off)
☐ Remove the wire from the sending unit and connect it to a good earth/ground on the engine.
☐ If this causes the light to come on, check for a bad connection at the sending unit. If the connection is good, replace the sending unit.
☐ If the light still doesn't come on, check the indicator bulb, socket and the wiring between the bulb and sending unit. If they check out OK, the problem is in the ignition switch or the wiring between the fuse panel and the light. **Note:** *Refer to the note at the beginning of this Section.*

### Engine coolant temperature light

#### The light comes on when the engine is operating
☐ Check the strength of the antifreeze, the radiator cap and the cooling system for leaks (refer to the Haynes Service and Repair Manual for your particular vehicle).
☐ If you know the cooling system is operating properly and the engine is not overheating, but the light still comes on when the engine is operating, check for a short to earth/ground in the wiring between the indicator light bulb and sending unit. If the wiring is OK, replace the sending unit.

#### The light does not operate
☐ The light should illuminate in the 'self test' mode (usually when the ignition key is turned to Start). If it doesn't, leave the ignition on (engine off), remove the wire from the sending unit and earth/ground it on the engine block. If the light now illuminates, check for a bad connection at the sending unit. If the connection is OK, replace the sending unit.
☐ If the light does not illuminate when the wire is earthed/grounded, check the bulb, bulb socket and wiring between the bulb and sending unit. If they check out OK, the problem is in the ignition switch or the wiring between the fuse panel and the light. **Note:** *Refer to the note at the beginning of this Section.*

## Electric gauge circuits

### Fuel gauges
There are two types of electrically operated fuel gauges – balancing-coil and thermostatic.

#### Balancing-coil type fuel gauges
Balancing coil systems consist of a sending unit and a gauge on the dash. Both units are connected in series by a wire to the battery (through the ignition switch). When the ignition switch is turned on, current from the battery flows through

*Typical balancing coil type fuel gauge system*

both the sending unit and gauge. The sending unit consists of a variable resistor and a sliding contact that's connected to a float lever. As the fuel level in the tank rises and falls, the float lever moves up and down, which in turn alters the position of the sliding contact on the variable resistor *(see illustration)*.

As the fuel level goes down, the float moves down too, and the sliding contact moves to reduce the resistance. So most of the current passing through the left-hand coil in the gauge flows through the resistor to ground. Little current flows through the right-hand coil, so the left-hand coil is magnetically stronger than the right-hand coil. The armature – and the pointer – thus swing to the left, and indicate a low fuel level.

When the fuel level is high, the float is up, and the sliding contact adds more resistance to the circuit. Therefore, most of the current going through the left-hand coil continues on through the right-hand coil. Thus the right-hand coil is relatively stronger and this causes the armature and pointer to swing toward the right, indicating a high fuel level.

## Thermostatic blade/variable resistor type fuel gauge

This type of thermostatic fuel gauge uses a variable resistor in the tank and a thermostatic blade in the gauge. The fuel sender unit in the tank has a resistor and a sliding contact that slides up and down as the float moves up and down. When it's up, indicating a full tank, the resistance is at a minimum, allowing maximum current to flow. This heats the thermostatic blade in the gauge to its maximum, causing it to warp and moving the needle to F (indicating a full tank). Note that this system doesn't use contact points that open and close.

This type of fuel gauge uses an instrument voltage regulator which is also thermostatic in operation. When the coil in the voltage regulator is connected to the battery, it heats up, causing the thermostatic blade to warp. As the blade warps, it opens the contact points, disconnecting the coil from the battery. The coil cools, the thermostatic blade straightens and the contact points close. The whole process is repeated. This action continues and keeps the voltage to the fuel-gauge system from increasing beyond the designed value *(see illustration)*.

*A typical blade/variable resistor type fuel gauge*

Note that the system also includes a radio choke and resistor. The voltage surges produced when the points open and close could cause radio interference. The choke coil and resistor smooth out the voltage surges and prevents this from happening.

## Oil pressure gauges

There are two types of electrically-operated oil pressure gauges: balancing-coil and bimetal thermostat type. Each type has two separate units. One is the sending unit on the engine; the other is the gauge on the dash.

On both types of gauges, the sending unit on the engine has a variable resistor and a moveable sliding contact *(see illustration)*. As pressure increases, a diaphragm moves up. This moves the contact along the resistor, which reduces the amount of current that can flow through the sending unit.

On a balancing-coil gauge, reducing the current flow through the sending unit strengthens the magnetism of the right-hand coil. That's because more of the current flowing through the left-hand coil flows through the right hand coil than through the sending unit. This pulls the armature, and the pointer, to the right *(see illustration)*.

The bimetal thermostat gauge contains a thermostatic bimetal strip with a small heater coil wrapped around it. As current flow through the sending unit changes, the amount of heat generated by the heater coil changes. This causes the bimetal strip to bend varying amounts to indicate the oil pressure *(see illustration)*. Normally, the voltage to a thermostatic gauge is controlled by an instrument voltage regulator, as described for fuel gauges (above).

*Here's an oil pressure sending unit used in a gauge-type system – note that it's much larger than sending units for indicator light systems, since it must house a variable resistor*

*A typical balancing coil type oil pressure gauge – bimetal thermostat type gauges use this same type sending unit but operate similarly to the blade/variable resistor type fuel gauge*

## Engine coolant temperature gauges

As with oil pressure gauges, there are two types of coolant temperature gauges: balancing-coil and bimetal thermostat. The circuits operate the same as their oil-pressure counterparts. Coolant temperature sending units for gauge circuits use a sensor that changes resistance as temperature changes (thermistor). The sending unit is immersed in engine coolant; its appearance and location are the same as a sending unit for a coolant temperature indicator light (see Indicator light circuits above).

Note that some vehicle manufactures use a sender unit which is not immersed in the engine coolant. Ford specifically, use a 'cylinder head temperature sensor'

*A typical bimetal thermostatic type engine oil pressure gauge*

**Ford cylinder head temperature sensor is _not_ immersed in coolant**

which screws into the aluminium casting of the cylinder head *(see illustration)*.

## Ammeters and voltmeters

An ammeter or voltmeter is used on some vehicles instead of, or in addition to, the charge warning light. Ammeters measure charging or discharging current in amperes, or 'amps.' Ammeters are wired between the alternator and the starter solenoid main power terminal.

Voltmeters indicate the voltage in the electrical system, which is usually a pretty good indication of the battery's state of charge. Voltmeters can be connected in parallel with any circuit that's switched off by the ignition switch.

## Troubleshooting a gauge circuit

Because of the low voltage and light current loads to which most gauges are subjected, they seldom malfunction or require any service. Even when they do appear to be broken, the trouble is more often than not in the sending unit. Usually, replacement of the sending unit solves the problem. **Note:** *Many late model vehicles have instrument clusters which have integral ECUs (Electronic control units) controlling the operation of the gauges. The ECUs have sophisticated self-diagnosis capabilities, and should be interrogated for any stored fault codes with a fault code reader via the diagnostic plug. before attempting any troubleshooting procedures. If faulty, the complete instrument cluster must often be replaced – check with your dealer.*

If you have more than one gauge and none of them is working, check the fuse.

If the gauges are all reading high, low or oscillating in unison, check for a faulty instrument voltage regulator (most of the time, one regulator controls all gauges) or a bad earth/ground connection for the gauge panel.

If one gauge is operating erratically, check for bad connections or a bad sending unit.

## Fuel gauges

One easy way to test a faulty fuel gauge is to substitute a fuel level sending unit of known accuracy. It isn't necessary to install the substitute unit in the tank. Simply disconnect the wire(s) from the unit in the tank and attach them to the same terminals on the test unit. Then connect a earth/ground wire between the test unit body and a good chassis earth/ground. Move the float arm through its entire range of motion and verify that this produces a consistent response from the gauge, with the needle moving from the Empty to Full positions.

If the gauge now operates properly, the old sending unit is bad. Remove it and check for a fuel-logged float, binding float or lack of continuity somewhere in the operating range of the float arm. Repair the unit, or replace it, as necessary. On some fuel gauges, you can shift the float or float arm to recalibrate the sending unit and correct the gauge reading. On others, you can shift the winding poles toward or away from the armature to recalibrate the gauge. You can clean dirty contact points – which cause needle fluctuation – on a gauge with vibrating thermostatic blades by pulling a strip of clean bond paper between them. Make sure that no particles of paper are left between the points.

> **⚠ *Caution: Never use emery cloth to clean the points – particles of emery will be embedded in the points and cause erratic gauge action.***

If the fuel gauge still doesn't register properly, either the gauge unit itself, or the wiring, is faulty. Check the wire between the sending unit and the fuel gauge for continuity. Check all wiring connections too. If the wiring and connections are okay, or if fixing any problem(s) with them doesn't give accurate readings, replace the fuel gauge.

## Temperature gauges

Disconnect the wire at the sending unit. The gauge should indicate Cold. Earth/ground the sending unit wire. The gauge should move to Hot. If the gauge operates as described with the sending unit wire disconnected and earth/grounded, but doesn't work properly when the wire is connected, replace the sending unit.

If the gauge indicates higher than Cold when the wire to the sending unit is disconnected, either the gauge is defective or there is a short to earth/ground somewhere in the wiring. Disconnect the wire that goes to the sending unit at the gauge. If the gauge now reads Cold, repair the wiring. Otherwise, replace the gauge.

If the gauge reads Cold when the wire is disconnected, but doesn't move to Hot when it's earthed/grounded, check the fuse (see Chapter 1). If the fuse is OK, earth/ground the sending unit terminal of the gauge. If this causes the gauge to read Hot, repair the wire that goes to the sending unit.

If there's no response from the gauge when the sending unit terminal is earthed/grounded, check for voltage at the ignition switch terminal on the gauge. If there's voltage and a good connection at the gauge, replace the gauge. If there's no voltage, the problem is in the ignition switch or the wiring between the fuse panel and the gauge.

## Oil pressure gauges

Since oil pressure gauge circuits are highly similar to temperature gauge circuits, the above procedure for temperature gauge circuits may also be used to troubleshoot oil pressure gauge circuits.

## Electronic instrumentation

All the gauge and indicator light circuits described thus far are electrical or electro-mechanical. In this section, we'll look at some typical electronic gauges.

### Electronic speedometer

Most early electronic speedometer circuits operate similarly. The speedometer receives an electrical signal representing vehicle speed from an optical sensor. Output from the optical sensor is generated by a slotted wheel, which is turned by a conventional mechanical speedometer cable connected to the speedometer drive gear in the transmission. Inside the optical sensor, a light emitting diode (LED) transmits a light beam at a light-sensitive transistor. The slotted wheel rotates in a plane perpendicular to this light beam. Each time the slotted part of the wheel allows the beam to pass through to the transistor, the transistor conducts a signal to the electronic speedometer. But when the solid part of the wheel interrupts the optical beam, the transistor ceases conducting. So the spinning wheel generates a steady series of pulses to the electronic speedometer. The number of pulses generated

are proportional to vehicle speed. Increasing the vehicle speed produces an increase in the pulse rate of the signal to the speedometer.

### Electronic fuel gauges

All electronic fuel gauges operate basically the same way. The voltage signal from a sending unit operates a horizontal or vertical bar display and, on most models, a low fuel warning light. The sending unit, located in the fuel tank, is similar in operation to the sending unit in thermostatic blade/variable resistor type electric gauge circuits (see above). Resistance from this sending unit varies the voltage sent to the gauge. The electronics in the gauge itself interpret the high or low voltage to display the appropriate gauge reading.

### Electronic temperature gauges

Electronic temperature gauges are similar in operation to electronic fuel gauges. A signal from a temperature sending unit immersed in engine coolant operates a horizontal bar display to indicate coolant temperature. Instead of a potentiometer in the sender unit, the temperature gauge system uses a thermistor (a resistor that changes resistance as the temperature changes). The thermistor used has a low resistance at high temperature and a high resistance at low temperature.

## Fitting a tachometer

Fitting a tachometer is a popular addition to the instrumentation fitted to slightly older cars. The following described the procedure applicable to the Vauxhall Nova, but applies generally to many models. Many such kits are available: check with your local car accessory shop or look on the internet.

*Decide where to located the tacho, and using the mounting bracket supplied, mark out where the holes need to be*

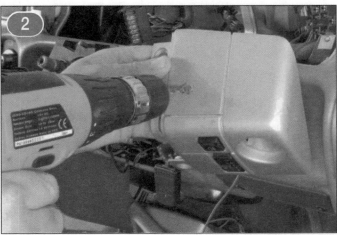

*Drill the holes for the bracket. Take care doing this – sticking on a piece of masking tape before marking/drilling helps stop the drill bit wandering off*

With the holes drilled, use the screws and nuts provided to attached the bracket to the facia

Then assemble the clamp for the gauge itself, which secures using a through-bolt

Then drill the hole for the wires to go through

In order to correct connect the tachometer, you need to find and identify a 12V live wire (when the ignition is switched on), and earth/ground, a tacho signal, and a live for the tacho illumination. Once identified, trim some of the insulation back using wire strippers or a sharp blade

With the wires stripped, you're ready to twist on the new wires and begin soldering

The ignition coil will have two low-tension connections – one is for power (12V with the ignition on), and the other is the signal wire. On this coil the signal side had a spare blade connection for us to use

With the new tacho signal connector in place, refit the coil low-tension connector

Fit the tachometer into the pod . . .

. . . and feed the wires down through the hole in the facia

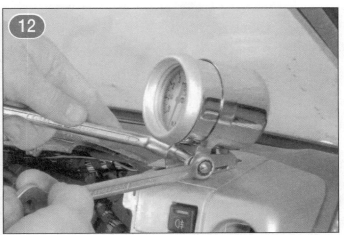

Angle the tacho as required, and tighten the clamp bolt

Feed the cable from the tacho to the wires already stripped/ prepared. Ensure the cable harness is safely routed, and secured in position using sufficient cable ties. With the wires prepared, twist on the connecting wires and begin soldering

Start the engine and check it's working

# Notes

# Accessories

## General information

In Chapters 1 and 3 we introduced you to basic circuits, troubleshooting and wiring repair. Now it's time to apply what you know to finding and correcting problems in accessory circuits.

The procedures that follow are by necessity general in nature. Whenever possible, supplement the information provided here with more specific procedures found in repair manuals written for the particular vehicle you are working on.

Before assuming an accessory circuit is faulty, be sure the battery has a reasonably good charge (see Chapter 4). Sometimes accessory circuits malfunction because they're not receiving sufficient voltage.

 *Caution: Never test solid-state components with battery voltage, test lights/buzzers or analogue multimeters. These devices may permanently damage electronic components.*

**Note:** *If the circuit in question keeps blowing fuses, check for a short circuit (see Chapter 3).*

# Chapter 8

## Cigarette lighters

Cigarette lighter circuits are among the simplest found on modern vehicles. They consist of one wire running from the fuse panel to the lighter socket, a heating element and an electrical ground return from the socket housing to the chassis.

Visually inspect the heating element and replace it if it appears damaged. Some lighters have a replaceable element that unscrews from the handle *(see illustration)*.

**Note:** *Some vehicles have the cigarette lighter wired through the ignition switch, so, when checking a cigarette lighter, always turn the ignition ON.*

### Troubleshooting

**1** Insert the lighter into the socket and allow time for it to heat. If it doesn't get hot, check the fuse (see Chapter 1).

**2** If the fuse is OK, probe the centre terminal in the socket with a test light, using the outer casing of the socket as a earth/ground for the light *(see illustration)*.

**3** If the test light lights, replace the heating element.

**4** If the test light doesn't light, connect the earth/ground wire to the ignition key (this is a good earth/ground on almost any vehicle). If the test light comes on now, repair the earth/ground connection on the lighter socket. Sometimes, the bad earth/ground is from a loose connection between the two parts of the socket *(see illustration)*.

**5** If the light still doesn't come on, trace the wiring back to the fuse panel and repair as necessary.

*Some lighters have a replaceable heating element which unscrews from the handle*

*Probe the centre terminal in the lighter socket with a test light*

*Some lighter sockets are composed of two parts which screw together*

*1 Earth/ground terminal    2 Positive terminal*

**A typical heater blower
wiring diagram**

1 Battery
2 Ignition switch
3 Battery fuse holder
4 Relay plate
91 'X' contact relay
123 Heater blower switch
124 Heater blower resistors
125 Fresh/recirculation air
flap motor
126 Heater blower motor

See diagram 12
interior lighting
(dimmed)

H45353

## Heater blowers

Heater circuits are relatively simple compared to the
complexity of most air conditioning systems. They all have a
blower motor, multi-position switch and resistor block. The
blower motor is wired in series with the switch resistor block.
For cooling, the resistor block is often mounted in the
blower airstream.

On most systems, current flows from the fuse panel to the
switch. Depending on which blower speed has been
selected, current is routed through different coils in the
resistor block, then through the blower motor to ground.

In 1980, Ford came out with a variation known as
earth/ground-side switching. On these systems current flows
from the fuse panel to the blower motor and then through
the switch and resistor block to earth/ground (see
illustration).

**A typical earth/ground-side switching wiring diagram**

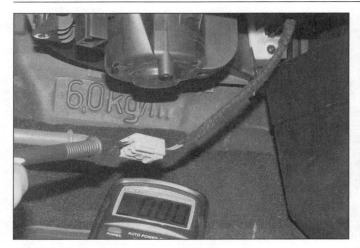

Checking for voltage going to the motor

Most vehicles have the blowers mounted either vertically or horizontally in the engine compartment on the passenger side (arrowed)

   Due to the large number of different systems available, the following instructions must be general in nature. You may have to obtain the wiring diagrams for the vehicle you are working on to solve some problems.

## Vehicles with the earth/ground at the blower motor

### The blower motor doesn't work at all

**1** Check the fuse (see Chapter 1).

**2** If the fuse is OK but the motor doesn't work, turn on the motor and check for voltage at the motor's positive connector *(see illustration)*. Most blower motors are located in the engine compartment on the bulkhead or under the facia behind the glove compartment *(see illustration)*. On some vehicles they are hidden under the scuttle panel in front of the windscreen *(see illustration)*.

**Note:** *The ignition must be On when checking for voltage.*

**3** If there's voltage at the motor, connect a jumper wire between the motor's earth/ground terminal (or case) and a good chassis earth/ground. Connect a fused jumper wire between the battery positive terminal and the positive terminal on the motor. If the motor now works, remove the jumper wire. If the motor stops working when the wire is removed, check for a bad earth/ground and retest. If the motor still doesn't work, replace it.

**4** If there's no voltage at the motor, remove the resistor block's connector and check it for voltage *(see illustration)*. If there's voltage at any of the connector terminals, check the resistor block and the wiring between the resistor block and the motor for an open or short circuit.

**5** If there's no voltage at any of the terminals in the resistor block's connector, remove the heater control panel (if necessary) and, with the ignition On, check for voltage at the

Some vehicles have the blower motor located under the scuttle, accessible from the engine compartment

The resistors electrical connector (A) and fixing screw (B) and cover (C)

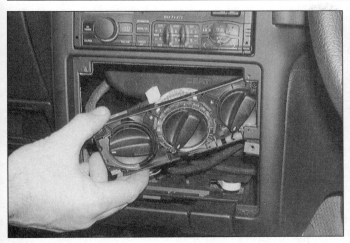

*To access the blower switch wiring, the heater control panel must usually be removed*

*Some vehicles use a relay (arrowed) to carry current when the blower is on high*

connector for the blower motor switch *(see illustration)*. If there's no voltage, check the wiring between the fuse panel and the switch for an open or a short circuit. If there's voltage, connect one end of a jumper wire to the terminal of the switch's connector with voltage. Connect the other end of the jumper to each of the terminals that carry voltage to the resistor block. If necessary, obtain the correct wiring diagram for the vehicle. If the motor now operates normally, replace the switch.

**6** If the motor does not operate with the control switch jumpered, check for an open or short circuit in the wiring from the switch to the resistor block.

### The motor only runs on high speed

**7** Remove the connector at the resistor block and check the resistor block for continuity. On most vehicles, there should be continuity between all the terminals. If you doubt the condition of the resistor block, remove it and check it visually.

**8** Test the blower motor switch as described in Step 5 above. If the motor works on other speeds when the switch is jumpered, replace the switch. If it still doesn't work on speeds other than high, check the wiring between the switch and the resistor block for opens and shorts.

### The motor only runs on low speeds but *not* on high speed

**9** Check for a blown inline fuse or a faulty high-speed relay – mostly on Vauxhall vehicles – (see Chapter 3) *(see illustration)*. If the inline fuse and relay (when equipped) are OK but the motor still doesn't work, check the blower switch, as described in Step 5. If the motor operates on high speed with the switch jumpered, replace the switch. If it doesn't, check the resistor block and the wiring between the switch and resistor block for short and open circuits.

## Vehicles with earth/ground-side switching

Use the following procedure when the blower motor does

not work at all. When the motor runs on high speed but not low speeds or on low speeds but not high speed, the procedures are the same as the ones above, except substitute Step 12 below when the procedures above refer you to Step 5.

**10** Check the fuse.

**11** With the ignition and blower motor switches on, check for voltage at the motor's positive connector. If there's no voltage, check the wiring between the fuse panel and the motor for an open or short. If there's voltage, test the motor, as described in Step 3.

**12** If the motor works when tested, remove the heater control panel (see Step 5 above) and use a jumper wire to earth/ground each terminal of the blower motor switch's connector. Make sure the ignition switch is on. If the motor now works, check for a bad earth/ground at the switch. If the switch's earth/ground is good, replace the switch.

**13** If the motor still doesn't work, remove the connector from the resistor block and earth/ground the connector terminal that leads to the earth/ground side of the blower motor. Make sure the ignition and blower switches are on. Obtain the correct wiring diagrams for the vehicle, if necessary. If the motor doesn't work, check for an open or short circuit in the wiring between the resistor assembly and the motor. If the motor works, check the resistor block and the wiring between the switch and resistor block for a short or open circuit.

## Electric rear view mirrors

Most electric rear view mirrors use two motors to move the glass; one for up and down adjustments and one for left-right adjustments. In addition, some mirrors have electrically heated glass defroster circuits, which are usually powered through the heated rear window relay.

*Mirror controls usually have a selector switch (arrowed) which sends power to the left or right mirror*

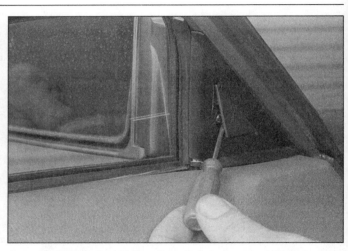

*On many modern vehicles, the mirrors are secured by screws on the inside of the door – remove the trim plate . . .*

*. . . to expose the mirror mounting screws*

## Troubleshooting

**1** The control switch usually has a selector portion which sends voltage to the left or right side mirror *(see illustration)*. With the ignition ON but the engine OFF, roll down the windows and operate the mirror control switch through all functions (left-right and up-down) for both the left and right side mirrors.

**2** Listen carefully for the sound of the electric motors running in the mirrors.

**3** If the motors can be heard but the mirror glass doesn't move, there's probably a problem with the drive mechanism inside the mirror. Remove and disassemble the mirror to locate the problem *(see illustrations)*.

**4** If the mirrors don't operate and no sound comes from the mirrors, check the fuse (see Chapter 1).

**5** If the fuse is OK, remove the mirror control switch from its mounting without disconnecting the wires attached to it *(see illustrations)*. Turn the ignition ON and check for voltage at

*On some vehicles the mirror switch panel prises up and slides out . . .*

*. . . whilst on others retaining screw(s) must be removed first (arrowed)*

the switch. There should be voltage at one terminal. If there's no voltage at the switch, check for an open or short circuit in the wiring between the fuse panel and the switch.

**6** If there's voltage at the switch, disconnect it. Obtain the correct wiring diagram for the vehicle and use it to check the switch for continuity in all its operating positions. If the switch does not have continuity, replace it.

**7** Re-connect the switch. Using the wiring diagram, locate the wire going from the switch to earth/ground. Leaving the switch connected, connect a jumper wire between this wire and earth/ground. If the mirror works normally with this wire in place, repair the faulty earth/ground connection.

**8** If the mirror still doesn't work, remove the mirror and check the wires at the mirror for voltage. Check with ignition ON and the mirror selector switch on the appropriate side. Operate the mirror switch in all its positions. There should be voltage at one of the switch-to-mirror wires in each switch position (except the neutral 'off' position).

**9** If there's not voltage in each switch position, check the wiring between the mirror and control switch for opens and shorts.

**10** If there's voltage, remove the mirror and test it off the vehicle with jumper wires *(see illustration)*. Replace the mirror if it fails this test.

*The mirror may be tested off the vehicle with fused jumper wires connected directly to the battery*

*A typical relay-type horn, showing its single terminal and adjustment screw (arrowed)*

## Horns

There are two basic designs for electric horn circuits; relay types and non-relay types *(see illustrations)*. Most vehicles use relays to handle the heavy current required by horns. If you aren't sure which type the vehicle has, study the wiring diagram.

### General troubleshooting

**1** If the horn is inoperative, check the fuse (see Chapter 1).
**Note:** *Some vehicles must have the ignition switch ON for the horn to work.*

**2** If the horn sounds weak, have an assistant operate the horn button while you listen at the front of the vehicle. Note whether the vehicle has multiple horns and determine if they are all working (touching each horn while its operating and feeling for a vibration is an easy way to do this).

**3** If a horn is weak or inoperative, check for a faulty earth/ground at the horn (relay-type systems) and check for full battery voltage going to the horn (do this with a voltmeter).

**4** If the horn tone is still poor, check for an adjustment screw and adjust for best tone.

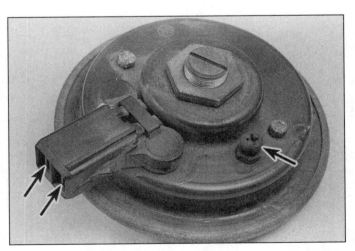
*A typical non-relay type horn, showing its two terminals and adjustment screw (arrowed)*

*A typical relay-type horn circuit diagram*

## Relay-type circuits

**5** When the horn button is depressed, the relay's control circuit is connected to earth/ground, which causes the horn relay to connect the horn(s) to the battery *(see illustration)*.

### The horn won't shut off

**6** Disconnect the horn(s), then check for a stuck horn button by disconnecting the button and re-connecting the horn(s) *(see illustration)*. If the horn is now silent, replace the horn

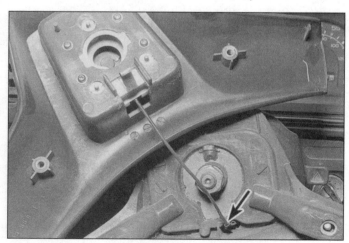

*This horn button is disconnected by first removing the steering wheel cover, then disconnecting the wire (arrowed)*

button. If the horn is still blowing, disconnect the wire that goes to the horn button at the relay. If that doesn't shut it off, replace the relay. If disconnecting the wire shuts off the horn, check the horn button wire for a short to earth/ground. **Note:** *On vehicles equipped with air bags, the driver's air bag module is usually integral with the horn control. It is essential that the air bag removal procedure specific to your vehicle is followed – refer to the appropriate Haynes Service and Repair Manual.*

### The horn doesn't work

**7** Check the fuse. If it's OK, check for voltage at the terminal on each horn when the horn button is depressed. If there's voltage at each terminal, check for a bad earth/ground at the horn(s). If the earth/ground is good, replace the horn(s).

**8** If there's no voltage at the horn(s), check the relay (see the relay check procedure in Chapter 3). Note that most horn relays are either the four-terminal or externally earthed/grounded three-terminal type.

**9** If the relay is OK, check for voltage to the relay's power and control circuits. If either of the circuits is not getting voltage, inspect the wiring between the relay and the fuse panel.

**10** If both relay circuits are receiving voltage, depress the horn button and check the wire that goes from the relay to the horn button for continuity to earth/ground. If there's no continuity, check the wire for an open circuit. If there's no open circuit in the wire, replace the horn button.

*A typical non-relay type horn circuit diagram*

*To check a non-relay type horn, disconnect the wires from the horn (arrowed) and connect fused jumper wires from the battery to the horn*

**11** If there's continuity to earth/ground through the horn button, check for an open or short circuit in the wire that goes from the relay to the horn(s).

### Non-relay type circuits

**12** On non-relay type horn circuits, voltage is connected directly from the fuse panel to the horn *(see illustration)*. The circuit is grounded through the horn button. This type circuit is used mostly on cars equipped with only one horn.

#### The horn won't shut off

**13** Disconnect the horn, disconnect the horn button, then reconnect the horn. If the horn is now silent, replace the horn button. If the horn is still sounding, check for a short circuit to earth/ground in the wire going from the horn to the horn button. **Note:** *On vehicles equipped with air bags, the driver's air bag module is usually integral with the horn control. It is essential that the air bag removal procedure specific to your vehicle is followed – refer to the appropriate Haynes Service and Repair Manual.*

#### The horn doesn't work

**14** If the general troubleshooting checks listed above don't find the problem, disconnect the horn and run power directly to the horn from the battery with fused jumper wires *(see illustration)*. If the horn doesn't work then, replace it.

**15** If the horn works with jumpers, check the wire that runs from the fuse panel to the horn for voltage at the horn. If there's no voltage, there's a short or open circuit between the fuse panel and the horn.

**16** If there's voltage at the horn, depress the horn button and check for continuity between earth/ground and the wire running from the horn to the horn button, with the wire disconnected from the horn. If there's no continuity, check the wire for an open circuit. If the wire's OK, replace the horn button.

## Electric door locks/central locking

Electric door lock systems are operated by bi-directional solenoids located in the doors. The lock switches have two operating positions: Lock and Unlock. These switches activate a relay which in turn connects voltage to the door lock solenoids. Depending on which way the relay is activated, it reverses polarity, allowing the two sides of the circuit to be used alternately as the feed (positive) and earth/ground side *(see illustration overleaf)*.

Due to the large number of systems available, we cannot supply detailed troubleshooting procedures for all types of vehicles. Some vehicles have keyless entry, electronic control modules and anti-theft systems incorporated into the power locks. If you are unable to locate the trouble using the following general steps, consult your a dealer service department or suitable equipped specialist. **Note:** *Some vehicles also have control switches connected to the key locks in the doors which unlock all the doors when one is unlocked.*

> **(!)** *Caution: Some late model vehicles are equipped with central locking systems that incorporate networks with a databus. These systems are equipped with a sophisticated self diagnosis system. Use a fault code reader to interrogate the system's ECU (Electronic control unit) for any stored fault codes, via the vehicles diagnosis connector. Do not attempt any traditional probing with a multimeter until the wiring diagrams have been studied and understood.*

### Troubleshooting

#### None of the power locks operate

**1** Always check the circuit protection first. Some vehicles use a combination of circuit breakers and fuses (see Chapter 1).

*A typical electric door lock circuit*

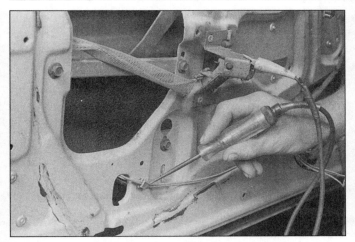

*Here a test light pierces the wire going to the solenoid, checking for voltage*

*Most door lock solenoids are bolted to the rear side of the door*

**2** Operate the door lock switches in both directions (Lock and Unlock) with the engine off. Listen for the faint click of the relay operating.

**3** If there's no click, check for voltage at the switches. If no voltage is present, check the wiring between the fuse panel and the switches for shorts and opens.

**4** If voltage is present but no click is heard, test the switch for continuity. Replace it if there's not continuity in both switch positions.

**5** If the switch has continuity but the relay doesn't click, check the wiring between the switch and relay for continuity. Repair the wiring if there's not continuity *(see illustration)*.

**6** If the relay is receiving voltage from the switch but is not sending voltage to the solenoids, check for a bad earth/ground at the relay case. If the relay case is earthing/grounding properly, replace the relay.

*After the bolts are removed, lift the solenoid out through the opening in the door and disconnect it*

**One power lock does not operate, but others**

**7** If all but one lock solenoids operate, remove the trim panel from the affected door and check for voltage at the solenoid while the lock switch is operated. One of the wires should have voltage in the Lock position; the other should have voltage in the unlock position.

**Note:** *For information on removing the trim panel, see the Haynes Service and Repair Manual for your particular vehicle.*

**8** If the inoperative solenoid is receiving voltage, replace the solenoid *(see illustrations)*.

**9** If the inoperative solenoid isn't receiving voltage, check for an open or short circuit in the wire between the lock solenoid and the relay.

**Note:** *It's common for wires to break in the portion of the harness between the body and door (opening and closing the door fatigues and eventually breaks the wires) (see illustration).*

*Wires often break inside the harness between the door and body (arrowed)*

# Chapter 8

## Electric windows

Electric windows are wired so they can be lowered and raised from the master control switch by the driver or by remote switches located at the individual windows. Each window has a separate motor which is reversible. The position of the control switch determines the polarity and therefore the direction of operation. Some systems are equipped with relays that control current flow to the motors.

Many vehicles are equipped with a separate circuit breaker for each motor in addition to the fuse or circuit breaker protecting the whole circuit. This prevents one stuck window from disabling the whole system.

Most electric window systems will only operate when the ignition switch is ON. In addition, many models have a window lockout switch at the master control switch which, when activated, disables the switches at the rear windows and, sometimes, the switch at the passenger's window also. Always check these items before troubleshooting a window problem.

Due to the large number of system types, these procedures are general in nature. If you can't find the problem using these procedures, take the vehicle to a dealer service department or auto electrical specialist.

*Check the switch for continuity in both directions*

### Troubleshooting

#### No windows work

**1** If the electric windows don't work at all, check the fuse or circuit breaker (see Chapter 1).

**2** If only the rear windows are inoperative, or if the windows only operate from the master control switch, check the rear window lockout switch for continuity in the unlocked position. Replace it if it doesn't have continuity.

**3** Check the wiring between the switches and fuse panel for continuity. Repair the wiring, if necessary.

#### One window is inoperative

**4** If only one window is inoperative from the master control switch, try the other control switch at the window.
**Note:** *This doesn't apply to the driver's door window.*

**5** If the same window works from one switch, but not the other, check the switch for continuity *(see illustration)*.

**6** If the switch tests OK, check for a short or open circuit in the wiring between the affected switch and the window motor *(see illustration)*.

**7** If one window is inoperative from both switches, remove the trim panel from the affected door and check for voltage at the motor while the switch is operated.
**Note:** *For information on removing the trim panel, check the Haynes Service and Repair Manual for your particular vehicle.*

**8** If voltage is reaching the motor, disconnect the glass from the regulator. Move the window up and down by hand while checking for binding and damage. Also check for binding and damage to the regulator *(see illustration)*. If the

*Checking for voltage going to the electric window motor*

*Here's a regulator and motor assembly removed from the vehicle – check for damage and binding at the points indicated by arrows*

regulator is not damaged and the window moves up and down smoothly, replace the motor *(see illustration)*. If there's binding or damage, lubricate, repair or replace parts, as necessary.

**9** If voltage isn't reaching the motor, check the wiring in the circuit for continuity between the switches and motors. You'll need to obtain the wiring diagram for the vehicle. Some electric window circuits are equipped with relays. If equipped, check that the relays are earthed/grounded properly and receiving voltage from the switches. Also check that each relay sends voltage to the motor when the switch is turned on. If it doesn't, replace the relay.

**10** Test the windows after you are done to confirm proper repairs.

## Power aerials

There are two basic types of power aerials: fully automatic and semi-automatic. Fully automatic antennas raise and lower when the radio is turned on or off. Semi-automatic types are raised or lowered by operating a dash-mounted switch.

The service life of an aerial may be increased by doing a little routine maintenance. Carefully clean off any accumulated dirt and grime from the mast with a soft, lint-free cloth. Some manufacturers recommend light lubrication of the mast to prevent sticking – check your owners manual for the proper procedure.

Most aerials have a drain hose coming from the bottom – inspect the hose to make sure it's not blocked.

Before checking for an electrical problem, inspect the mast. A bent or damaged mast is the most common cause of a stuck aerial. Bent masts usually can't be straightened successfully. Some models have replaceable masts. Check with a dealer. When replacing a mast, be sure to follow the instructions provided with the new mast. If the mast isn't replaceable, the whole aerial may have to be replaced *(see illustration)*.

If the following general procedures do not identify your aerial problem, take the vehicle to a dealer service department or auto electrical specialist for further diagnosis.

### Troubleshooting

**1** If the aerial doesn't work at all, check the fuse (see Chapter 1).

**2** Operate the aerial with the ignition ON but the engine OFF. Listen for the sound of the aerial motor.

**3** If the mast doesn't move but the motor runs, remove the aerial assembly inspection cover and check for a broken mast *(see illustration)*.

**4** If the motor doesn't run, have an assistant operate the aerial control while you check for voltage and earthing/grounding at the aerial. If the aerial has a good earth/ground and is getting voltage, it's faulty – replace it.

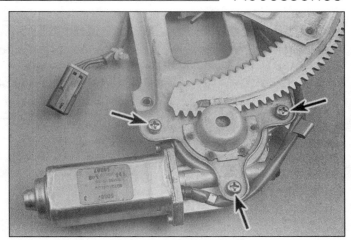

*This typical motor is secured to the regulator by three screws (arrowed) – you may have to remove the regulator assembly before you can remove the motor*

*Some aerial masts may be replaced without removing the aerial from the vehicle*

*Sometimes the plastic leader portion of the mast (arrowed) breaks off inside the power aerial housing*

*A typical power aerial wiring diagram*

**5** If the aerial isn't getting voltage, check for voltage at the relay. If the relay's receiving voltage, check for a bad earth/ground at the relay and check that the relay's sending voltage to the aerial when the aerial control is turned on. If the relay's receiving voltage but not sending it to the aerial, replace the relay *(see illustration)*.

**6** If the relay isn't getting voltage, check the wires going to the relay for a short or open circuit.

**7** On semi-automatic models, check for voltage at the switch and check the switch for continuity in both the UP and DOWN positions. If the switch does not have continuity in both directions, replace the switch. If there's no power to the switch, check the wiring between the fuse panel and the switch for a short or open circuit.

**8** On fully automatic models, if there's voltage at the radio but no voltage going from the radio to the relay with the radio turned on, you'll normally have to remove the radio and have it checked by a qualified radio repair workshop.

*Checking for voltage at the aerial connector*

## Heated rear window

Electric heated rear windows function by passing an electric current through thin conductors mounted on the inner surface of, or moulded into, the rear window glass. The demister circuit on most vehicles includes a fuse or circuit breaker, a timer relay, switch, warning lamp, rear window grid and connecting wiring *(see illustration)*. On some vehicles, the timer relay also controls current to defrosters on the outside rear-view mirror glass.

### Troubleshooting

**1** Check the fuse and replace it, if necessary (see Chapter 1).

**2** With the ignition ON (engine OFF), switch ON the heated rear window with the driver's door open. The interior (courtesy) light should dim considerably.

**3** If the interior light dims when the heated rear window is

switched ON, check the rear window for damaged grid lines (see below).

**4** If the light doesn't dim, check for a bad connection at the window grid. If the connections are OK, trace the circuit and

*A typical heated rear window circuit*

*There may be two connections on the window grid – to find out which one is positive, probe them with a test light – if it lights, you've found the positive connector*

*A test light may be used to find the 'dead' portions of the window grid*

check continuity of the switch and of the wiring from the fuse panel to the switch/relay and from the relay to the rear window. Repair or replace as necessary.

**5** If the circuits and switch have continuity, replace the relay.

**6** The heated rear window should stay ON for about 10 minutes before the timer relay shuts it OFF (check your owners manual). If the heated rear window won't stay ON for the specified time, replace the relay.

**Note:** *On some modern vehicles, the function of the heated rear window timer is incorporated into a central timer unit. This unit is responsible for providing timing facilities for all the vehicle's systems (indicators, wipers, etc.).*

## Checking and repairing the rear window grid

**Note:** *The following procedure applies only to grids attached to the surface of the window. Some vehicles have the grid **inside** the glass. On these vehicles, you must replace the window to repair a faulty grid.*

**7** Visually inspect the edges of the rear window grid for missing or broken wires or bad connections.

**8** Start the engine and turn the heated rear window switch ON. Allow several minutes for the glass to warm up.

**9** Verify operation by holding your hand against the glass in the grid area to feel for warmth or by watching the ice or fog disappear from the window. If the glass only warms up in certain areas, the grid may have open segments.

**10** The specific grid lines that are open may be determined by noting which ones don't demist. You can normally mist the glass by breathing on it.

**11** Locate the open spot in the grid line by looking for a small gap in the line. If the gap is invisible, use a test light to find it. Starting at the positive side of the grid, touch the test light to the grid line at various points along the line. When you reach a point where the test light no longer lights, the gap lies between that point and your last test point *(see illustrations).*

**12** Mark the damaged spot with a crayon or tape on the outside of the glass. The grid lines may be repaired with a

special kit available from dealers and car accessory shops *(see illustration).* Follow the instructions provided in the kit *(see illustration).*

**Note:** *Large breaks in the grid require window replacement.*

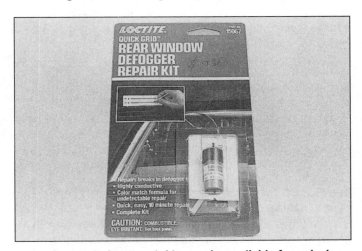

*Heated rear window repair kits maybe available from dealers and car accessory shops*

*To use a heated rear window repair kit, apply masking to the inside of the window at the damaged area, then brush on the special conductive coating*

*Washer nozzles can often be carefully cleaned out with a pin or straightened paper clip*

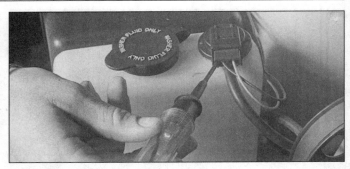

*Checking for voltage at the washer pump*

## Windscreen washers

Most windscreen washer systems are equipped with a small electric motor-driven pump located on or adjacent to the windscreen washer fluid reservoir. These are commonly known as rotary vane pumps.

Fluid is pumped through hoses and lines to one or two nozzles located on the bonnet, on the cowl in front of the windscreen or on the windscreen wipers themselves.

### General troubleshooting

**1** Check the washer fluid level. If it's OK, turn on the washer pump with the ignition switch ON, but the engine OFF. Listen for the sound of the pump operating. You should hear a whirring sound. If you can't hear the pump operating, proceed to the troubleshooting procedure below.

**2** If you can hear the pump operating but no fluid is being expelled from the washer nozzles, trace the hoses and lines between the pump and nozzles to be sure there's none kinked, damaged or disconnected.

**3** If the hoses and lines are OK, disconnect a hose as close to a nozzle as possible and operate the washer again. If a strong stream of fluid is expelled from the end of the hose, the nozzle is probably clogged. Often, nozzles can be unclogged by inserting a pin or paper clip into the hole in the end *(see illustration)*. If this doesn't unclog the nozzle, replace it. **Note:** *Take great care not to damage the washer jet with the pin of paper clip.*

**4** If there's no fluid being expelled from the hose, trace it back to the pump and disconnect it there. Operate the washer again. If a strong stream of fluid is expelled from the pump, there's a blockage in the line between the pump and nozzle(s). If no fluid is expelled from the pump, but you can hear it operating, replace it.

**5** If there's no sound coming from the pump when it's turned on, have an assistant operate the washer button (ignition ON) while you check for voltage and earth/ground at the pump *(see illustration)*. If there's voltage and a good earth/ground, but the pump doesn't work, replace the pump.

**6** If voltage isn't getting to the pump, check the switch and wiring for continuity and repair as necessary.

## Windscreen wipers

Wiper systems come with multiple speeds. In addition, some have an interval mode for light rain and drizzle. Most wiper switches also have a function which controls the windscreen washer pump. When the washer switch is operated, the wipers

*A typical multi-speed wiper circuit diagram*

| | | |
|---|---|---|
| 1 | Battery | |
| 2 | Ignition switch | |
| 3 | Battery fuse holder | |
| 4 | Relay plate | |
| 9 | Fuse holder | |
| 129 | Wash/wipe switch | |
| 130 | Washer pump | |
| 131 | Wash/wipe relay | |
| 132 | Wiper motor | |
| 133 | Wiper delay rheostat | |

are switched on to clear the windscreen. **Note:** *On some modern vehicles, the function of the interval timer is incorporated into a central timer unit/generic electronic module. This unit is responsible for providing timing facilities for all the vehicles systems (indicators, heated rear window, etc.).*

The major components of the wiper system are the control switch, the wiper motor assembly, washer fluid pump (see the previous Section) and interval control module or central timer unit (on vehicles with interval wipers only) *(see illustration)*.

Wiper motors have built-in limit switches that allow the wiper arms to park at the bottom of the windscreen every time the wipers are shut off. The limit switch has voltage to it whenever the ignition is ON. Some vehicles have an additional function that reverses the wiper motor during the park phase to stow the wiper arms out of sight below the bonnet line.

There are many variations in circuitry among the manufacturers. It is recommended that you obtain the specific wiring diagram for the vehicle you are working on. The following information is by necessity general in nature. If you are unable to locate and correct the problem using the following procedures, take the vehicle to a dealer service department or automotive electrical specialist.

## Troubleshooting

### The wipers work slowly

**1** Make sure the battery is in good condition and has a strong charge (see Chapter 4).

**2** Remove the wiper motor and operate the wiper arms by hand. Check for binding linkage and pivots. Lubricate or repair the linkage or pivots, as necessary.

### The wipers don't work at all

**3** Check the fuse or circuit breaker (see Chapter 1).

**4** If the fuse or circuit breaker is OK, connect a jumper wire between the wiper motor and earth/ground, then retest. If the motor works now, repair the earth/ground connection *(see illustration)*.

**5** If the wipers still don't work, turn on the wipers and check for voltage at the motor. If there's voltage at the motor, remove the motor and check it off the vehicle with fused jumper wires from the battery *(see illustration)*. If the motor now works, check for binding linkage (see Step 2 above). If the motor still doesn't work, replace it.

**6** If there's no voltage at the motor, check for voltage at the switch. If there's no voltage at the switch, check the wiring between the switch and fuse panel for continuity. If there's voltage at the switch, check the wiring between the switch and motor for continuity.

> ⓘ *Caution: If the vehicle you are working on has an interval mode, use a digital ohmmeter for continuity checks – other devices may damage the solid state circuitry in the control module.*

*A common cause of wipers not working is a bad earth/ground at the wiper motor – look for corrosion or looseness around the earth/ground connection (arrowed)*

*To remove a typical wiper motor, unplug the wiring connector, remove the bolts (arrowed) and pull the motor out far enough to disconnect the linkage behind it*

**7** If the wiring is OK, obtain a wiring diagram for the circuit and use it to check the continuity of the switch. Replace the switch, if necessary.

### The wipers only work on one speed

**8** Check the continuity of the wires between the switch and motor. If the wires are OK, replace the switch.

### The interval function is inoperative

**9** Check the continuity of all the wiring between the switch and motor. If the wiring is OK, replace the interval module. **Note:** *On some modern vehicles, the function of the interval timer is incorporated into a central timer unit. This unit is responsible for providing timing facilities for all the vehicles systems (indicators, heated rear window, etc.). These units*

# Chapter 8

are equipped with sophisticated self diagnostic facilities. Use a fault code reader to interrogate the unit for any stored fault codes, via the vehicle's diagnostic connector.

### The wipers stop wherever they are when the switch is shut off (fail to park)

**10** Check for voltage at the wiper motor when the wiper switch is OFF but the ignition is ON. If voltage is present, the limit switch in the motor is malfunctioning. Replace the wiper motor. If no voltage is present, trace and repair the limit switch wiring between the fuse panel and wiper motor.

### The wipers won't shut off unless the ignition is OFF

**11** Disconnect the wiring from the wiper control switch. If the wipers stop, replace the switch. If the wipers keep running, there's a defective limit switch in the motor. Replace the motor.

### The wipers won't retract below the bonnet line (vehicles equipped with this function)

**12** Check for mechanical obstructions in the wiper linkage or on the vehicle's body which would prevent the wipers from retracting.

**13** If there are no obstructions, check the wiring between the switch and motor for continuity. If the wiring is OK, replace the wiper motor.

## Fitting an aftermarket parking assistance system

Parking assistance systems have been available as factory-fitted options for a number of years. However, they are also available as a DIY kit which is straightforward to fit, and inexpensive to buy.

The systems all work on the well established ultrasound technology, and have several sensors fitted to the rear (and sometimes the front also), of the vehicle. Normally these sensors are recessed into the bumper cover(s). The sensors send and receive ultrasonic waves, which bounce off obstacles. The time delay between sending and receiving the ultrasonic signal is proportional to the distance from the sensor to the obstacle.

The driver is informed of the distance to the obstacle by an audible signal and sometimes a visual display as well. The sound is emitted by a buzzer or loudspeaker. A typical audible signal will increase in frequency as the vehicle approaches the obstacle, and eventually a continuous tone as contact becomes imminent (e.g. within 25 cm). The visual display can take the form of an LED display, normally above the rear windscreen, built into the rear view mirror, or an LCD display which indicates the actual distance to the obstacle.

**Note:** *If the following instructions contradict in any way those supplied with your kit, follow the ones supplied by the kit's manufacturer.*

*Check the contents of the kit and read the instructions thoroughly. Plan ahead to work out where the various system components are to fitted*

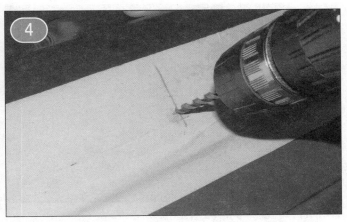

Use a ruler and mark exactly where the sensors are to be fitted, depending on which type you have

Using a drill of the appropriate size, drill the holes for the sensors. The drill bit needs to be just big enough to allow the sensors to be pushed into place. With the type of sensors we fitted, the hole size was 20.0 mm, but check with the instructions/sensors you have – there are several different types

Using a felt-tip pen or pencil, mark the proposed position of the sensors on the rear bumper. We used masking tape on the bumper so that the marks would show up without marking the bumper surface

With the positions marked out, it's time to drill some holes. Because we were unsure of what lay immediately behind, we removed the bumper to be on the safe side. Make sure there are no brackets or other obstructions behind the bumper for the sensors to foul

If the correct drill bit size is not available, drill a smaller pilot hole, and enlarge it to the correct size using a small round file or hole expander

Remove any burrs from the edges of the holes

*Depending on which type of sensor you're using, they may need to be fitted a certain way up. Ours needed to be fitted with the thinnest part of the sensor rim uppermost (note the arrow)*

*Push the sensors into place, then if necessary, seal them in place using silicone sealant. Avoid getting any sealant onto the 'face' of the sensor, and don't use glue – it may damage the sensors*

*With all the sensors fitted, decide where to fit the central control unit. You need to bear in mind the length of the cables from the sensors. Our control unit was secured in place using the double-sided self-adhesive pad supplied with the kit. Make sure the surface for the pad to stick to is clean and free from grease*

*We fitted the unit behind the side panel trim in the passenger compartment. Make sure it's not likely to be damaged by any goods etc. being carried if it's fitted in the luggage compartment, and it's close enough to the wiring loom for the reversing lights*

*Identify the reversing light wire by turning the ignition on, selecting reverse, and probing the connector at the reversing light with a test bulb or meter*

*With the wire identified, trace the cable/loom to the nearest point to the central control unit. Joint the cable supplied to the reversing light wire using the snap-splice connector provided*

Find a suitable earth connection for other wire to the central control unit. You may be able to splice into an existing earth wire nearby, or make your own earth point by drilling a hole in the car body, and using a self-tapping screw and an eyelet crimp connector

Determine the best route for the sensor's wiring harness. Try not to run the loom over any sharp edges. Where possible, make use of any existing cable holes that use rubber grommets

It's often possible to push additional cables through the grommet. Secure the harness in place using the cables ties provided

To make pulling the loom through easier, tape it together in several places along its length. Take care not to damage the connectors when you're pull the loom through

Connect the various wiring plugs to the central control unit

Note that the cables from the sensors are labelled to correspond with the appropriate sockets on the control unit – eg. middle left to middle left etc. At this point it's worth connecting the display unit and audible warning speaker (where supplied), then turning on the ignition and selecting reverse to make sure the system works. If the system doesn't function correctly, follow the troubleshooting procedures detailed in the instructions supplied with the kit

Identify the most suitable position for the audible warning speaker (where supplied), and the visual display unit. We used a mobile phone bracket on the facia . . .

. . . to mount the LCD screen . . .

. . . and we used a double-sided adhesive pad to position the speaker adjacent to the passenger glovebox on a bracket under the facia

Run the cables behind the various pieces of trim. Ensure that the cable is routed so that it doesn't chafe on any sharp edges, and secure it in place with cable ties

Then check the system still works!

# Glossary

## A

**Active material**
The material on the negative and positive battery plates that interacts with the electrolyte to produce a charge.

**AC generator**
An electromechanical device that generates alternating current (AC), commonly known as an alternator. Usually belt-driven off the engine. Provides maximum output at relatively low rpm. Used on all modern vehicles. Requires a rectifier to convert AC to direct current (DC), which is used by automotive electrical system.

**Aftermarket parts**
Components that can be added to a vehicle after its manufacture. These parts are often accessories and should not be confused with original equipment manufacturer (OEM) service or replacement parts.

**Alligator clip**
A long-nosed spring-loaded metal clip with meshing teeth. Used to make temporary electrical connections. Often also known as a Crocodile clip

**Alloy**
A mixture of two or more materials.

**Alternating current (AC)**
An electric current, generated through magnetism, whose polarity constantly changes back and forth from positive to negative.

**Alternator**
A device used in automobiles to produce electric current. The alternator's AC output is rectified to direct current before it reaches the vehicle's electrical system.

**Ammeter**
An instrument for measuring current flow. An ammeter can be designed to measure alternating or direct current.
An instrument panel gauge used to measure the flow rate of current into or out of the battery. The ammeter is calibrated in amperes for both charge and discharge rates, in ranges of 20, 30 or more amperes.

**Amperage**
The total amount of current (amperes) flowing in a circuit.

**Ampere (amp)**
The unit of measurement for the flow of electrons in a circuit. The amount of current produced by one volt acting through a resistance of one ohm (1 coulomb per second).

# Glossary

**Ampere hour**

A unit of measurement for battery capacity, obtained by multiplying the current (in amperes) by the time (in hours) during which the current is delivered.

**Analogue gauge**

see 'gauge.'

**Analogue signal**

A signal which varies in exact proportion to a measured quantity, such as pressure, temperature, speed, etc.

**Arcing**

When electricity leaps the gap between two electrodes, it is said to be 'arcing.'

**Armature**

The rotating part of a generator or motor. Actually a coil of wires wrapped in a specific pattern, which rotates on a shaft.

**Atoms**

The small particles which make up all matter. Atoms are made up of a positive-charged nucleus with negative-charged electrons whirling around in orbits.

# B

**Battery**

A group of two or more cells connected together for the production of an electric current by converting chemical energy into electrical energy. A battery has two poles positive and negative. The amount of positive and negative energy is called potential.

**Battery charging**

The process of energising a battery by passing electric current through the battery in a reverse direction.

**Battery ratings**

Performance standards conducted under laboratory conditions to describe a battery's reserve capacity and cold-crank capacities. The amp-hour rating is no longer in widespread use. See 'cold crank rating.'

**Battery state of charge**

The available amount of energy in a battery in relation to that which would ordinarily available be if the battery was fully charged.

**Battery voltage**

A figure determined by the number of cells in a battery. Because each cell generates about two volts, a six cell battery has 12 volts.

**Bendix inertia drive**

A self-engaging and releasing starter drive mechanism. The pinion gear moves into engagement when the starter motor spins and disengages when the engine starts.

**Bound electron**

An electron whose orbit is near the nucleus of an atom and is strongly attracted to it.

**Brush**

A spring-loaded block of carbon or copper that rubs against a commutator or slip ring to conduct current. A key component in all alternators and starters.

**Bulkhead connector**

An OEM device used to connect wiring inside the vehicle body with wiring outside the body. Usually located at the bulkhead or firewall.

**Butt connector**

A solderless connector used to permanently join two wire ends together.

**Bypass**

A shunt, or parallel path, around one or more elements in a circuit.

# C

**Cable**

An assembly of one or more conductors, usually individually insulated and enclosed in a protective sheath.

**Capacity**

The current output capability of a cell or battery, usually expressed in ampere hours.

**Cell**

In a storage battery, one of the sets of positive and negative plates which react with electrolyte to produce an electric current.

**Central timer unit (CTM)**

Electronic module fitted to some Ford models, which provides timing functions for various electrical system (intermittent wipers, heater windscreens, courtesy lights, etc.).

**Charge**

A definite quantity of electricity.

**Charge (recharge)**

To restore the active materials in a battery cell by electrically reversing the chemical action.

**Circuit**

An electrical path from the source (battery or generator) through the load (such as a light bulb) and back to the source through which current flows. A typical circuit consists of a battery, wire, load (light or motor) and switch. See 'simple circuit' and 'single-wire circuit.'

**Circuit breaker**

A circuit-protection device that automatically opens or breaks an overloaded circuit. The typical circuit breaker usually consists of movable points that open if the preset ampere load is exceeded. Some circuit breakers are self-resetting; others require manual resetting.

**Closed circuit**

A circuit which is uninterrupted from the current source, through the load and back to the current source.

**Closed-end connector**

Solderless connector shaped like a hat. Used to join two, three or more wires together. Similar to wire connectors used in home wiring, but installed by crimping instead of twisting.

**Clutch interlock switch**

A switch that prevents the vehicle from starting unless the clutch is pressed.

**Coil**

Any electrical device or component consisting of wire loops wrapped around a central core. Coils depend on one of two electrical properties for operation, depending on the application (electromagnetism or induction).

**Cold-crank rating**

The minimum number of amperes a fully charged 12-volt battery can deliver for 30 seconds at -17° C (0° F) without falling below 7.2 battery volts.

**Commutator**

A series of copper bars insulated from each other and connected to the armature windings at the end of the armature. Provides contact with fixed brushes to draw current from (generator) or bring current to (starter) the armature.

**Conductance**

A measure of the ease with which a conductor allows electron flow. In DC circuits, conductance is the reciprocal of resistance.

**Conduction**

The transmission of heat or electricity through, or by means of, a conductor.

**Conductor**

Any material usually a wire or other metallic object made up of atoms whose free electrons are easily dislodged, permitting easy flow of electrons from atom to atom. Examples are copper, aluminium and steel. Conductors are all metals. The metal part of an insulated wire is often called the conductor.

**Constant voltage regulator (CVR)**

A device used to maintain a constant voltage level in a circuit, despite fluctuations in system voltage. CVRs are wired into some gauge circuits so voltage fluctuations won't affect accuracy of the gauge readings.

**Contact**

One of the contact-carrying parts of a relay or switch that engages or disengages to open or close the associated electrical circuits.

**Continuity**

A continuous path for the flow of an electrical current.

**Conventional theory**

In this theory, the direction of current flow was arbitrarily chosen to be from the positive terminal of the voltage source, through the external circuit, then back to the negative terminal of the source.

**Coulomb**

The unit of quantity of electricity or charge. The electrons that pass a given point in one second when the current is maintained at one ampere. Equal to an electrical charge of $6.25 \times 10^{18}$ electrons passing a point in one second. See 'ampere.'

**Current**

The movement of free electrons along a conductor. In automotive electrical work, electron flow is considered to be from positive to negative. Current flow is measured in amperes.

**Cycle**

A recurring series of events which take place in a definite order.

# D

**DC generator**

An electromechanical device that generates direct current. Usually belt-driven off the engine. Because the DC generator requires high rpm for maximum output, it's no longer used in production automobiles.

**Deep cycling**

The process of discharging a battery almost completely before recharging.

**Digital gauge**

See 'gauge.'

**Diode**

A semiconductor which permits current to flow in only one direction. Diodes are used to rectify current from AC to DC.

**Direct current (DC)**

An electrical current which flows steadily in only one direction.

**Discharge**

Generally, to draw electric current from the battery. Specifically, to remove more energy from a battery than is being replaced. A discharged battery is of no use until it's recharged.

# Glossary

**Disconnect terminal**

Solderless connectors in male and female forms, intended to be easily disconnected and connected. Typically, a blade or pin (male connector) fits into a matching receptacle or socket (female connector). Many components have built-in (blade) terminals that require a specialised female connector.

**Display**

Any device that conveys information. In a vehicle, displays are either lights, gauges or buzzers. Gauges may be analogue or digital.

**DPDT**

A double-pole, double-throw switch.

**DPST**

A double-pole, single-throw switch.

**Draw**

The electric current required to operate an electrical device.

**Drive**

A device located on the starter to allow for a method of engaging the starter to the flywheel.

# E

**Earth**

The connection made in earthing a circuit. In a single-wire system, any metal part of the car's structure that's directly or indirectly attached to the battery's negative post. Used to conduct current from a load back to the battery. Self-earthed components are attached directly to an earthed metal part through their mounting screws. Components mounted to non-earthed parts of a vehicle require an earth wire attached to a known good earth. Also known as Ground.

**Electric**

A word used to describe anything having to do with electricity in any form. Used interchangeably with electrical.

**Electrical balance**

An atom or an object in which positive and negative charges are equal.

**Electricity**

The movement of electrons from one body of matter to another.

**Electrochemical**

The production of electricity from chemical reactions, as in a battery.

**Electrolyte**

A solution of sulphuric acid and water used in the cells of a battery to activate the chemical process which results in an electrical potential.

**Electromagnet**

A soft-iron core which is magnetised when an electric current is passed through a coil of wire surrounding it.

**Electromagnetic**

Having both electrical and magnetic properties.

**Electromagnetism**

The magnetic field around a conductor when a current is flowing through the conductor.

**Electromechanical**

Any device which uses electrical energy to produce mechanical movement.

**Electrons**

Those parts of an atom which are negatively charged and orbit around the nucleus of the atom.

**Electron flow**

The movement of electrons from a negative to a positive point on a conductor, or through a liquid, gas or vacuum.

**Electron theory**

States that all matter is made up of atoms which are made up of a nucleus and electrons. Free electrons moving from one atom to another, in a single direction, produce what is known as electricity.

**Electronics**

The science and engineering concerned with the behaviour of electrons in devices and the utilisation of such devices. Especially devices utilising electron tubes or semiconductor devices.

**Energy**

The capacity for performing work.

**EVR**

Electronic Voltage Regulator; a type of regulator that uses all solid state devices to perform the regulatory functions.

# F

**Field**

An area covered or filled with a magnetic force. Common terminology for field magnet, field winding, magnetic field, etc.

**Field coil**

A coil of insulated wire, wrapped around an iron or steel core, that creates a magnetic field when current is passed through the wire.

**Filament**

A resistance in an electric light bulb which glows and produces light when an adequate current is sent through it.

**Fluorescent**

Having the property of giving off light when bombarded by electrons or radiant energy.

**Flux**

The lines of magnetic force flowing in a magnetic field.

**Flywheel**

A large wheel attached to the crankshaft at the rear of the engine.

**Flywheel ring gear**

A large gear pressed onto the circumference of the flywheel. When the starter gear engages the ring gear, the starter cranks the engine.

**Free electron**

An electron in the outer orbit of an atom, not strongly attracted to the nucleus; it can be easily forced out of its orbit.

**Fuse**

A circuit-protection device containing a soft piece of metal which is calibrated to melt at a predetermined amp level and break the circuit.

**Fuse block**

An insulating base on which fuse clips or other contacts are mounted.

**Fuse link**

See 'fusible link.'

**Fuse panel**

A plastic or fibreboard assembly that permits mounting several fuses in one centralised location. Some fuse panels are part of, or contain, a terminal block (see 'terminal block').

**Fuse wire**

A wire made of an alloy which melts at a low temperature.

**Fusible link**

A circuit protection device consisting of a conductor surrounded by heat-resistant insulation. The conductor is two gauges smaller than the wire it protects, so it acts as the weakest link in the circuit. Unlike a blown fuse, a failed fusible link must often be cut from the wire for replacement.

# G

**Gassing**

The breakdown of water into hydrogen and oxygen gas in a battery.

**Gauge**

A standard SAE designation of wire sizes, expressed in AWG (American Wire Gage). The larger the gage number, the smaller the wire. Metric wire sizes are expressed in cross-sectional area, which is expressed in square millimetres.

**Gauge**

An instrument panel display used to monitor engine conditions. A gauge with a movable pointer on a dial or a fixed scale is an analogue gauge. A gauge with a numerical readout is called a digital gauge. Also refers to measuring device used to check regulator point openings.

**Generator**

An engine-driven device that produces an electric current through magnetism by converting rotary motion into electrical potential (see 'AC generator' and 'DC generator').

**Generic electronic module (GEM)**

Electronic module which provides control functions for various electrical systems (direction indicator lights, hazard warning lights, interior lights, heated windscreens, windscreen washers/wipers, seat belt warnings, door ajar warning, central locking, anti-theft alarm, etc.).

**Grid**

A lead screen that is pasted with active materials to form a negative or positive battery plate.

**Grommet**

A doughnut shaped rubber or plastic part used to protect wiring that passes through a panel, firewall or bulkhead.

**Ground**

The connection made in grounding a circuit. In a single-wire system, any metal part of the car's structure that's directly or indirectly attached to the battery's negative post. Used to conduct current from a load back to the battery. Self-grounded components are attached directly to a grounded metal part through their mounting screws. Components mounted to non-grounded parts of a vehicle require a ground wire attached to a known good ground. Also known as Earth.

# H

**Halogen light**

A special bulb that produces a brilliant white light. Because of its high intensity, a halogen light is often used for fog lights and driving lights.

**Harness**

A bundle of electrical wires. For convenience in handling and for neatness, all wires going to a certain part of the vehicle are bundled together into a harness.

**Harness ties**

Self-tightening nylon straps used to bundle wires into harnesses. Available in stock lengths that can be cut to size after installation. Once tightened, they can't be removed unless they're cut from the harness.

**Harness wrap**

One of several materials used to bundle wires into manageable harnesses. See 'loom,' 'split loom,' 'loom tape' and 'harness ties').

**Hot**

Connected to the battery positive terminal, energised.

**Hydrogen gas**

The lightest and most explosive of all gases. Emitted from a battery during charging procedures. This gas is very dangerous and certain safety precautions must be observed.

# Glossary

**Hydrometer**

A syringe-like instrument used to measure the specific gravity of a battery's electrolyte.

## I

**Ignition switch**

A key-operated switch that opens and closes the circuit that supplies power to the ignition and electrical system.

**Indicator light**

An instrument-panel display used to convey information or condition of the monitored circuit or system. See 'warning light.'

**Induced**

Produced by the influence of a magnetic or electrical field.

**Induced current**

The current generated in a conductor as it moves through a magnetic field, or as a magnetic field is moved across a conductor.

**Induced voltage**

The voltage produced as a result of an induced current flow.

**Inductance**

That property of a coil or other electrical device which opposes any change in the existing current, present only when an alternating or pulsating current is flowing. Has no effect on the flow of direct, or static, current.

**Induction**

The process by which an electrical conductor becomes charged when near another charged body. Induction occurs through the influence of the magnetic fields surrounding the conductors.

**Input**

The driving force applied to a circuit or device.

The terminals (or other connection) where the driving force may be applied to a circuit or device.

**Instrument Voltage Regulator**

See 'Constant Voltage Regulator.'

**Insulator**

A material that has few or no free electrons that readily leave their orbits. A non-conducting material used for insulating wires in electrical circuits. Cloth, glass, plastic and rubber are typical examples. Wires for modern vehicles use plastic insulation.

**Integral**

Formed as a unit with another part.

**Intercell connector**

A lead strap or connector that connects the cells in a battery.

**Intermittent**

Coming or going at intervals; not continuous.

**Ion**

An atom having an imbalanced charge due to the loss of an electron or proton. An ion may be either positively charged (have a deficiency of electrons) or negatively charged (have a surplus of electrons).

## J

**Jumper**

A short length of wire used as a temporary connection between two points.

**Junction**

A connection between two or more components, conductors or sections of transmission line.

Any point from which three or more wires branch out in a circuit.

**Junction box**

A box in which connections are made between different cables.

## L

**Lead-acid battery**

A common automotive battery in which the active materials are lead, lead peroxide and a solution of sulphuric acid.

**Lead dioxide**

A combination of lead and oxygen, as found in the storage battery. Lead dioxide is reddish brown in colour.

**Lead sulphate**

A combination of lead, oxygen and sulphur, as found in the storage battery.

**Light**

An electrical load designed to emit light when current flows through it. A light consists of a glass bulb enclosing a filament and a base containing the electrical contacts. Some lights, such as sealed beam headlights, also contain a built-in reflector.

**Load**

Any device that uses electrical current to perform work in a vehicle electrical system. Lights and motors are typical examples.

**Loom**

A harness covering. Older vehicles used woven-cloth loom; most modern vehicles use a corrugated-plastic loom or split loom.

**Loom tape**

A non-adhesive tape used as a harness wrap. Adhesive-type tapes, including electrical tapes, are not recommended for wrapping harnesses. Often, a piece of shrink wrap is used at tape ends to keep the tape from unravelling.

# M

**Magnet**
A material that attracts iron and steel. Temporary magnets are made by surrounding a soft-iron core with a strong electromagnetic field. Permanent magnets are made with steel.

**Magnetic field**
The field produced by a magnet or a magnetic influence. A magnetic field has force and direction.

**Magnetic poles**
The ends of a bar or horseshoe magnet.

**Magnetism**
A property of the molecules of certain materials, such as iron, that allows the substance to be magnetized.

**Meter**
An electrical or electronic measuring device.

**Module**
A combination of components packaged in a single unit with a common mounting and providing some complete function.

**Motor**
An electromagnetic apparatus used to convert electrical energy into mechanical energy.

**Multimeter**
A test instrument with the capability to measure voltage, current and resistance.

# N

**Negative charge**
The condition when an element has more than a normal quantity of electrons.

**Negative ion**
An atom with more electrons than normal. A negative ion has a negative charge.

**Negative terminal**
The terminal on a battery which has an excess of electrons. A point from which electrons flow to the positive terminal.

**Neutral**
Neither positive nor negative, or in a natural condition. Having the normal number of electrons, i.e. the same number of electrons as protons.

**Neutral start switch**
On vehicles with an automatic transmission, a switch that prevents starting if the vehicle is not in Neutral or Park. Often referred to as a Starter Inhibitor Switch.

**Neutron**
A particle within the nucleus of an atom. A neutron is electrically neutral.

**Nichrome**
A metallic compound containing nickel and chromium, used in making high resistances.

**North pole**
The pole of a magnet from which the lines of force are emitted. The lines of force travel from the north to the south pole.

**Nucleus**
The core of an atom. The nucleus contains protons and neutrons.

**Nylon ties**
See 'harness ties.'

# O

**OEM (Original Equipment Manufacturer)**
A designation used to describe the equipment and parts installed on a vehicle by the manufacturer, or those available from the vehicle manufacturer as replacement parts. See 'aftermarket parts.'

**Ohm**
The practical unit for measuring electrical resistance.

**Ohmmeter**
An instrument for measuring resistance. In automotive electrical work, it's often used to determine the resistance that various loads contribute to a circuit or system.

**Ohm's Law**
The electrical formula that describes how voltage, current and resistance are related. The basic formula is E (electrical pressure in volts) = I (current flow in amperes) x R (resistance in ohms). What does it mean? Simply put, amperage varies in direct ratio to voltage and in inverse ratio to resistance.

**Open circuit**
An electrical circuit that isn't complete because of a broken or disconnected wire.

**Open circuit voltage**
The battery voltage when the battery has no closed circuit across the posts and is not delivering or receiving voltage.

**Orbit**
The path followed by an electron around the nucleus.

**Output**
The current, voltage, power or driving force delivered by a device or circuit. The terminals or connections where the current can be measured.

**Overrunning clutch**
A device located on the starter to allow for a method of engaging the starter with the flywheel. The overrunning clutch uses a shift lever to actuate the drive pinion to provide for a positive meshing and de-meshing of the pinion with the flywheel ring gear.

# Glossary

## P

**Parallel circuit**
A method or pattern of connecting units in an electrical circuit so that they're connected negative-to-negative and positive-to-positive. In a parallel circuit, current can flow independently through several components at the same time. See 'series circuit.'

**Permanent magnet**
A magnet made of tempered steel which holds its magnetism for a long period of time.

**Pinion**
A small gear that either drives or is driven by a larger gear.

**Plate**
A battery grid that's pasted with active materials and given a forming charge which results in a negative or positive charge. Plates are submerged, as elements, in the electrolyte and electricity is produced from the chemical reactions between the plates and the electrolyte.

**Polarity**
The quality or condition of a body which has two opposite properties or directions; having poles, as in an electric cell, a magnet or a magnetic field.

**Polarity-protected connector**
A multiple-cavity connector that can be connected in only one way, either to a mating connector or to a component.

**Pole**
A positive (or negative) terminal in a cell or battery; the ends of a magnet (north or south).

**Pole shoe**
The part of a starter that's used to hold the field coils in place in their proper positions; consists of a soft-iron core which is wound with heavy copper ribbons.

**Positive**
Designating or pertaining to a kind of electrical potential.

**Positive terminal**
The battery terminal to which current flows.

**Post**
A round, tapered battery terminal that serves as a connection for battery cables.

**Potential**
Latent, or unreleased, electrical energy.

**Power supply**
A unit that supplies electrical power to a unit. For example, a battery.

**Printed circuit**
An electrical conductor consisting of thin metal foil paths attached to a flexible plastic backing. Also called a PC board. PC boards are used primarily in OEM instrument clusters and other electronic devices.

**Proton**
A positively-charged particle in the nucleus of an atom.

## Q

**Quick charger**
A battery charger designed to allow the charging of a battery in a short period of time.

## R

**Rectification**
The process of changing alternating current to direct current.

**Rectifier**
A device in the electrical system used to convert alternating current to direct current.

**Regulator**
A device used to regulate the output of a generator or alternator by controlling the current and voltage.

**Relay**
An electromagnetic device that opens or closes the flow of current in a circuit.

**Resistance**
The resistance to electron flow present in an electrical circuit, expressed in ohms.

**Resistor**
Any conductor that permits electron movement but retards it. Tungsten and nickel are typical resistors.

**Rheostat**
A variable resistor, operated by a knob or handle, used to vary the resistance in a circuit. A rheostat consists of a coil of resistance wire and a movable contact or wiper that creates more or less resistance in the circuit, depending on how many coil windings it allows the current to pass through. The dimmer control for instrument panel illumination is an example.

**Ring terminal**
A conductor used to attach a wire to a screw or stud terminal. The ring is sized to the mating screw. Ring terminals are the connectors least likely to vibrate loose in rugged applications. Comes in soldered and unsoldered versions.

**Rotor**
That part of an alternator which rotates inside the stator.

## S

**Schematic**
A drawing system for portraying the components and wires in a vehicle's electrical system, using standardised symbols.

**Secondary**
The output winding of a transformer, i.e. the winding in which current flow is due to inductive coupling with another coil called the primary.

**Sending unit**

Used to operate a gauge or indicator light. In indicator light circuits, contains contact points, like a switch. In gauge circuits, contains a variable resistance that modifies current flow in accordance with the condition or system being monitored. Also known as a Sender Unit.

**Separator**

A thin sheet of non-conducting material that is placed between the negative and positive plates in an element to prevent the plates from touching.

**Series circuit**

A circuit in which the units are consecutively connected or wired positive to negative and in which current has to pass through all components, one at a time.

**Series/parallel circuit**

A circuit in which some components are wired in series, others in parallel. An example: Two loads wired in parallel with each other, but in series with the switch that controls them.

**Short circuit**

An unintentional routing of a current, bypassing part of the original circuit.

**Shorted winding**

The winding of a field or armature that's earthed/grounded because of accidental or deliberate reasons.

**Shrink wrap**

An insulating material used to protect wire splices and junctions at terminals. Upon application of open flame or heat, the wrap shrinks to fit tightly on the wire or terminal. Also known as Heat Shrink.

**Shunt**

Connected in parallel with some other part.
A precision low value resistor placed across the terminals of an ammeter to increase its range.

**Simple circuit**

The simplest circuit includes an electrical power source, a load and some wire to connect them together.

**Single-wire circuit**

Generally used in production vehicles, in which one wire brings current to the load and the vehicle's frame acts as the return path (earth/ground).

**Slip ring**

A device for making electrical connections between stationary and rotating contacts.

**Snap-splice connector**

Solderless connector used to tap an additional wire into an existing wire without cutting the original. Often used when installing accessories.

**Solder**

An alloy of lead and tin which melts at a low temperature and is used for making electrical connections.

**Solderless connector**

Any connector or terminal that can be installed to a wire without the use of solder. They're usually crimped in place using a special crimping tool. Ring terminals, spade terminals, disconnect terminals, butt connectors, closed-end connectors and snap-splice connectors are typical examples. Ring and spade terminals also come in soldered versions.

**Solenoid**

An electromechanical device consisting of a tubular coil surrounding a movable metal core, or plunger, which moves when the coil is energised. The movable core is connected to various mechanisms to accomplish work.

**Spade terminal**

A terminal used to connect a wire to a screw or stud terminal. The spade terminal has two forked ends, either straight or with upturned tips. They're more convenient to install than ring terminals, but slightly less secure for rugged applications. Comes in soldered and unsoldered versions.

**SPDT**

A single-pole, double-throw switch.

**Specific gravity**

The measure of a battery's charge, made by comparing the relative weight of a volume of its electrolyte to the weight of an equal volume of pure water, which has an assigned value of 1.0. A fully charged battery will have a specific gravity reading of 1.260. See 'hydrometer.'

**Split loom**

Flexible, corrugated conduit used to bundle wires into harnesses.

**SPST**

A single-pole, single-throw switch.

**Starter**

A device used to supply the required mechanical force to turn over the engine for starting.

**Stator**

In an alternator, the part which contains the conductors within which the field rotates.

**Sulphuric acid**

A heavy, corrosive, high-boiling liquid acid that is colourless when pure. Sulphuric acid is mixed with distilled water to form the electrolyte used in storage batteries.

**Supply voltage**

The voltage obtained from the power supply to operate a circuit.

**Switch**

An electrical control device used to turn a circuit on and off, or change the connections in the circuit. Switches are described by the number of poles and throws they have. See 'SPST, SPDT, DPST and DPDT.'

# Glossary

## T

**Tachometer**

A device that measures the speed of an engine in rpm. Also known as a Rev Counter.

**Terminal**

A device attached to the end of a wire or to an apparatus for convenience in making electrical connections.

**Terminal block**

A plastic or resin assembly containing two rows of terminals screws. Used to join the circuits in several wiring harnesses.

**Test light**

A test instrument consisting of an indicator light wired into the handle of a metal probe. When the probe contacts a live circuit, current flows through the light, lighting it, and to ground through an attached lead and alligator clip. Used to test for voltage in live circuits only.

**Test light (self-powered)**

A test device containing an indicator light and a built-in battery. Used to test continuity of circuits not containing voltage at the time of the test. Used to test continuity in a harness before it's installed in the vehicle. Also called a continuity tester.

**Thermal relay**

A relay actuated by the heating effect of the current flowing through it.

**Thermistor**

The electrical element in a temperature sending unit that varies its resistance in proportion to temperature. Unlike most electrical conductors, in which resistance increases as temperature rises, resistance in a thermistor decreases. Thermistors are made from the oxides of cobalt, copper, iron or nickel.

**Tracer**

A stripe of a second colour applied to a wire insulator to distinguish that wire from another one with the same colour insulator.

**Transformer**

An apparatus for transforming an electric current to a higher or lower voltage without changing the total energy.

## V

**Variable resistor**

A wire-wound or composition resistor with a sliding contact for changing the resistance. See 'rheostat.'

**Variable transformer**

An iron-core transformer with a sliding contact which moves along the exposed turns of the secondary winding to vary the output voltage.

**Volt**

A practical unit for measuring current pressure in a circuit; the force that will move a current of one ampere through a resistance of one ohm.

**Voltage drop**

The difference in voltage between two points, caused by the loss of electrical pressure as a current flows through an impedance or resistance. All wire, no matter how low the resistance, shows at least a trace of voltage drop.

**Voltage regulator**

An electromechanical or electronic device that maintains the output voltage of a device at a predetermined value.

**Voltmeter**

A test instrument that measures voltage in an electrical circuit. Used to check continuity and determine voltage drop in specific circuits of vehicle electrical systems.

An instrument panel gauge that measures system voltage. When the engine's not running, the voltmeter indicates battery voltage, which should be 12 to 13 volts in a 12-volt system. When the engine's running, the voltmeter indicates total system voltage, or the combined voltage output of the alternator and the battery.

**VOM (Volt-Ohmmeter)**

A two-in-one test instrument. For convenience, a voltmeter and an ohmmeter are mounted in the same case and share a common readout and test leads.

## W

**Warning light**

An instrument panel display used to inform the driver when something undesirable has happened in the monitored circuit or system, such as an overheated engine or a sudden loss of oil pressure.

**Watt**

The unit for measuring electrical energy or 'work.' Wattage is the product of amperage multiplied by voltage.

**Winding**

One or more turns of a wire, forming a coil. Also, the individual coils of a transformer.

**Wire**

A solid or stranded group of cylindrical conductors together with any associated insulation.

## X

**Xenon**

An inert gas used in high performance lighting bulb.